SRA Spelling Mastery

Workbook

Level F

Robert Dixon

Siegfried Engelmann

Donald Steely

Tina Wells

Columbus, OH

The McGraw·Hill Companies

Cover Photo Credit: Getty Images, Inc.
Illustrations: Janice Skivington

SRAonline.com

 **SRA**

Copyright © 2007 by SRA/McGraw-Hill.

Printed in the United States of America.

Send all inquiries to:
SRA/McGraw-Hill
4400 Easton Commons
Columbus, OH 43219

ISBN 0-07-604486-6

11 12 13 14 QLM 15 14

Lesson 1

A

Their report showed great imagination.

Their report shows great imagination.

B

1. acquire
2. deport
3. requirement
4. eksport
5. suported
6. portable
7. imquire

inquire

exsport

supported

C

In most words the morphograph **port** means "to carry." A port is a place where ships or airplanes pick up things and carry them away. If something is portable, it can be carried. A portable television is one that you can carry. The word **portable** is made of the morphographs **port** and **able**.

Port means "to carry." **Able** means "can be." So the word **portable** means "can be carried."

Things that are imported are carried into countries or places. The word **import** is made of the morphographs **im** and **port**.

Im means "in." **Port** means "to carry." So the word **import** means "to carry in."

In some words the meaning of **port** is more difficult to see. The word **important** comes from the word **import**. A long time ago the things imported into countries were very valuable. These things were called **important**, which means they were valuable. Later the word **important** came to mean "having great value."

1. The morphograph **er,** which means "one who," is often added to the end of words. What word would mean **"one who carries things"?**

   Porter

2. A foundation of a building is **under** the building. It **carries** the weight of the building. These morphographs mean under: **sub, suc, sup, sur, sug, suf.** Which one goes with the morphograph **port** to tell what a foundation does for the rest of the building?

   Support

3. Goods **carried out of** a country are exported. What does the morphograph **ex** mean?

   out of

4. **Trans** means "across." What word means **"carry across land or water"?**

   Transport

D

Write the morphographs for each word.

1. ___Port___ + ___able___ = portable
2. ___un___ + ___re___ + ___port___ + ___ed___ = unreported
3. ___in___ + ___quire___ = inquire
4. ___tele___ + ___graph___ = telegraph
5. ___Photo___ + ___graph___ + ___ic___ = photographic
6. ___ac___ + ___quire___ = acquire

Lesson 2

A

Their report showed great imagination. ✓

B

Write the morphographs for each word. If you are not sure of a spelling, use Word Parts.

1. _Photo_ + _graph_ + _er_ ✓ = photographer
2. _mis_ + _in_ + _form_ + _ed_ ✓ = misinformed
3. _in_ + _form_ + _al_ ✓ = informal
4. _per_ + _form_ + _ance_ ✓ = performance
5. _re_ + _quire_ ✓ = require
6. _im_ + _port_ + _ant_ ✓ = important

C

The morphograph **port** means "to carry." Below are some words that use the morphograph **port**.

1. **export:** When goods are carried out of a country, those goods are exported.

2. **portable:** Something that can be carried is portable.

3. **transport:** When you transport something, you carry it across land, water, or air.

4. **support:** When you support something, you carry the weight or hold it up.

5. **important:** Something that is valuable is important.

6. **airport:** An airport is a place where things are carried in or out by aircraft.

7. **report:** When you report on something, you carry information back.

Use the words with **port** to complete these sentences.

1. Maria said she wants to talk with you right away. She said it's very
   __important__ .

2. Japan does not import half as many things as it __exports__ .

3. Kim wants to __transport__ the packages by train, but I think they would
   arrive sooner if they were shipped by air.

4. My television is too big to take with me wherever I go. I would rather have a
   __portable__ television.

5. The building is going to collapse unless we can __support__ the
   first floor.

6. My flight leaves in an hour. Can you drive me to the __airport__ ?

7. He wrote a __telegraph__ on Spain that was very informative.
   Report

D

1. misspell   photograph
2. morphograph   telegraph
3. photograf   mistaken
4. telagraph
5. misstaken
6. misjudged

E

1. t __C__   4. l __C__   7. p __C__   10. o __V__
2. e __V__   5. u __V__   8. a __V__   11. b __C__
3. n __C__   6. i __V__   9. d __C__   12. e __V__

Lesson 3

A

Their report showed great imagination

B

1. a __V__ ✓
2. c __C__ ✓
3. i __V__ ✓

4. s __C__ ✓
5. u __V__ ✓
6. d __C__ ✓

7. p __C__ ✓
8. v __C__ ✓
9. e __V__ ✓

10. u __V__ ✓
11. n __C__ ✓
12. t __C__ ✓

C

1. replace + ing = replacing ✓
2. replace + ment = replacement ✓
3. forgive + en = forgiven ✓
4. like + ly = likely ✓
5. use + age = usage ✓
6. change + ing = changing ✓
7. use + ful = useful ✓
8. like + ness = likeness ✓
9. wide + est = widest ✓
10. trace + ing = tracing ✓
11. bare + ly = barely ✓
12. reuse + able = reusable ✓

D

1. The first morphograph in the word **introduce** is either **in** or **intro.** Use Word Parts to find the correct morphograph. Then write the morphographs.

   ___intro___ + ___duce___ ✓ = introduce

2. The first morphograph in the word **across** is either **a** or **ac.** Use Word Parts. Then write the morphographs.

   ___ac a___ + ___cross___ ✗ = across

3. The last morphograph in the word **action** is either **tion** or **ion.** Use Word Parts. Then write the morphographs.

   ___act___ + ___tion___ ✓ = action

4. The first morphograph in the word **wonderful** is either **won** or **wonder.** Use Word Parts. Then write the morphographs.

   ___Wonder___ + ___full___ ✓ = wonderful

E

Three of these words are misspelled. Use Word Parts if you are not sure of the correct spellings. Write the misspelled words correctly on the lines.

1. formmal   _formal_
2. telegraph
3. reformed   _acquire_
4. akquire
5. transsport   _transport_
6. greatly

Lesson 4

A

1. Their photographs showed no imagination.
2. We gave a report on her great preformance.

B

1. hope + ing = hoping
2. hope + ful = hopeful
3. late + ly = lately
4. decide + ed = decided
5. expense + ive = expensive
6. love + ly = lovely
7. mistake + en = mistaken
8. require + ment = requirement
9. fine + al = final
10. fame + ous = famous

C

1. The second morphograph in the word **fortunate** is either **un** or **une**. Use Word Parts to find the correct morphograph. Then write the morphographs.

   fort + un + ate = fortunate

2. The second morphograph in the word **discontent** is either **con** or **co**. Use Word Parts.

   dis + con + tent = discontent

3. The last morphograph in the word **uncover** is either **er** or **cover**. Use Word Parts.

   un + cover = uncover

4. The second morphograph in the word **television** is either **vise** or **vis**. Use Word Parts.

   tele + vis + ion = television

D

 snap   art   civil   trim

likely	morphograph	introduce	requirement
should	misspell	performance	usable
telegraph	acquire	transmit	support
forgiven	television	really	translate
useful	photographic	imagination	important
reported	formal	misinformed	hopelessly
	great	inquire	

F

The morphograph **graph** means "something in writing" or "something that is drawn." Below are some words that use the morphograph **graph.**

biography: Bio means "life." When you write a story about someone's life, you write a biography.

autobiography: Auto means "self." An autobiography is a biography you write about yourself.

morphograph: Morpho means "the form of something." So a morphograph is the written form of a word part.

autograph: Another word for your signature is your autograph.

graph: A graph is a drawing or a chart.

graphic: If something is graphic, it is like a graph. A drawing is a graphic. When you describe something in graphic detail, your description is as clear as a drawing.

Write the morphographs for each word.

1. _____graph_____ + ___ic___ = graphic
2. _____bio_____ + ___graph___ + ___y___ = biography
3. _____auto_____ + ___graph___ = autograph
4. __auto__ + __bio__ + __graph__ + __y__ = autobiography
5. What does the morphograph **auto** mean? __by itself__

Write the correct words containing **graph.**

6. After she became rich and famous, she wrote her ___autobiography___.
7. I asked a film star to write her __autograph__ inside my book.
8. Gil read a __biography__ about Winston Churchill.
9. They described the play in __graphic__ detail.

Lesson 5 is a test lesson.
There is no worksheet.

Lesson 6

A

1. (plan)
2. rest
3. winter
4. (big)
5. (step)
6. port
7. brother
8. (ship)
9. earn

B

Use Word Parts to find the correct morphographs for each word. Write the morphographs below.

1. The last morphograph in the word **surprise** is either **ise** or **prise.**

   ___Sur___ + ___prise___ = surprise

2. The last morphograph in the word **interest** is either **est** or **rest.**

   ___inter___ + ___est___ = interest

C

In Lesson 4 you learned that the morphograph **graph** refers to something in writing or something that is drawn. Here are other words that contain **graph.**

graphite: Pencil lead is graphite.

telegraph: The morphograph **tele** means "distance." A telegraph sends messages over long distances.

photograph: The morphograph **photo** means "light." Photographs are pictures made with light.

geography: The morphograph **geo** means "earth." When you study geography, you study drawings or maps of Earth.

bibliography: The morphograph **biblio** means "book." A list of books used in writing an article is called a bibliography.

Write the morphographs for each word.

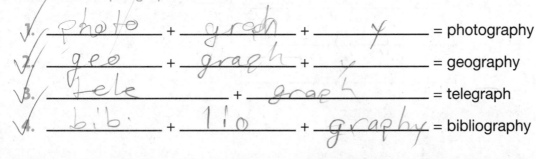

1. ___photo___ + ___graph___ + ___y___ = photography
2. ___geo___ + ___graph___ + ___y___ = geography
3. ___tele___ + ___graph___ = telegraph
4. ___bib___ + ___lio___ + ___graphy___ = bibliography

Answer the items.

5. What does the morphograph **photo** mean? _picture X light_

6. What does the morphograph **tele** mean? _distance_

7. I am learning a lot about Earth's surface in my _geography_ class.

8. The word **photo** is a shorter word for _photograph_.

9. The lead in my pencil is made of _graphite_.

10. There is a long _bibliography_ at the end of the book.

D

Add the morphographs together. Remember to use the final-**e** rule.

1. change + ing   = _changing_

2. trade + s   = _trades_

3. tele + scope   = _telescope_

4. con + fuse + ion = _confusion_

5. value + able   = _valuable_

6. base + ment   = _basement_

E

Four of these words are misspelled. Use Word Parts if you are not sure of the correct spellings. Write the misspelled words correctly on the lines.

1. geographer   _civilize_
2. preformance
3. across   _hopelessly_
4. civelize
5. hopelesly   _autograph_
6. transmit
7. replacement   _performance_
8. autograf

Lesson 7

A

I admire conscientious people.

B

criticism   pleasure   notice   stranger   translation

C

Add the morphographs together. Remember to use the doubling rule.

1. part + ing = parting
2. pat + ing = patting
3. bag + age = baggage
4. knot + s = knots
5. form + al = formal
6. mad + ness = madness
7. pack + age = package
8. got + en = gotten

D

    Last Saturday, my family went to see a new play. It was realy bad. A man interduced the play before it startted. He said we would have to use our imaginasions, but the play was hopeles.

    All the actors gave terrible preformances. Nobody understood the story. I wish we had stayed home and watched teluvision.

really
introduced
started
imaginations
hopeless
performances
television

E

Use Word Parts to find the correct morphographs for each word. Write the morphographs below.

1. The first morphograph in the word **pleasure** is either **please** or **plea.**

   _____please_____ + _____ure_____ = pleasure

2. The second morphograph in the word **transmission** is either **miss** or **mis.**

   _____trans_____ + _____miss_____ + _____ion_____ = transmission

3. The first morphograph in the word **dispel** is either **dis** or **di.**

   _____dis_____ + _____pel_____ = dispel

F

Add the morphographs together. Remember to use the final-**e** rule.

1. pulse + ate   = _pulsate_

2. in + quire + ing = _inquiring_

3. white + est   = _whitest_

4. base + ic   = _basic_

5. ex + press + ive = _expressive_

6. athlete + ic   = _athletic_

7. value + less   = _valueless_

8. store + age   = _storeage_

Lesson 8

A

I admire conscientious people.

B

partial   athletically   deduction   excessively   critically

C

Add the morphographs together. Remember to use the doubling rule.

1. sad + ness = _Sadness_
2. wash + er = _washer_
3. spot + ed = _spoted_
4. magic + al = _magical_
5. hat + s = _hats_
6. critic + ism = _criticism_
7. trip + ed = _tripped_
8. civil + ize = _civilize_

D

The origin of a word is the place the word originally came from. The word **tea** originally came from China, which is where people first got tea leaves. The Chinese word for tea is **tay.** When English people took over the word, they changed the word to **tea.** Many English words have foreign origins, like the word **tea.** But very few words come from Chinese.

Most English words follow the same pattern of origin. These words were first in Greek. Then they went to Latin. Then they went to French. And finally, they became part of English. Greek is the language spoken in Greece and is over three thousand years old. Latin is the language that people used to speak in Italy. French is the language that people speak in France.

The Greeks were very smart. They made up many words and ideas. The people in Italy admired the Greeks and copied what they did. Italian people often copied Greek words. They changed the words a little bit, but the Latin words were clearly copies of the Greek words.

When people from Italy moved into France, they took the Latin language with them. The French people changed the Latin words and changed the spelling.

When these words come into English, they are Greek words that have been changed somewhat when they went into Latin and changed again when they went into French. Sometimes their spelling and pronunciation change again as the word becomes an English word.

1. Where was Latin spoken? _____ *Italy* _____

2. Where is French spoken? _____ *France* _____

3. Is Latin still spoken today? _____ *no* _____

4. What is the origin of a word? _____ *it is where the word comes from* _____

5. Where does the word **tea** come from? _____ *it comes from china* _____

6. From whom did the Italians copy words? _____ *The greek people* _____

E

A student wrote this letter. The letter contains nine misspelled words. Write each of those words correctly. If you're not sure of a word, look it up in Word Parts.

Dear Grandmother,

Last Friday was the last day of shcool, so our famly will be comming to visit you soon. On Friday, we had a spelling contest in our class, and my best freind won! I did okay at first, but the spelings got too hard, and I made a misstake trying to spell ATHLETIC, so I was out of the contest. Connie did'nt mispell a single word, including the last one, which was DINOSAUR, so she won a realy nice dictionary.

See you next week!

Love,
Bernice

family

coming

friend

spellings

mistake

didn't

really

misspell

school

Lesson 9

A

I admire conscientious people.

B

1. _____ 4. _____
2. _____ 5. _____
3. _____ 6. _____

C

admirable   medicine   physicist   amusement   photography

D

Write the morphographs for each word. Figure out any morphographs you don't know. Use Word Parts.

1. fort + __un__ + __ate__ = fortunate
2. in + __ver__ + __sion__ = inversion
3. __tele__ + __vis__ + ion = television
4. per + __cep__ + __tive__ = perceptive
5. __critic__ + __al__ + ly = critically

E

Four of these words are misspelled. Use Word Parts to find the correct spellings. Write the misspelled words correctly.

1. finaly   __finally__
2. unbreakable
3. partial   __performance__
4. preformance
5. intermission   __supervision__
6. atheletically
7. excessively   __atheticaly__
8. deduction
9. supervizion

Add the morphographs together. Remember to use the doubling rule.

1. sit + ing   = _sitting_
2. wonder + ful = _wonderfull_
3. real + ize   = _realize_
4. snap + ed   = _snapped_
5. star + less   = _starless_
6. swim + er   = _swimmer_
7. hot + est   = _hottest_
8. poison + ous = _poisonous_

People who lived in Italy used to speak Latin. Those people were called Romans. The Romans used the Roman alphabet to spell Latin words. The 26-letter English alphabet comes from the Roman alphabet. The Roman alphabet comes from the 24-letter Greek alphabet.

So a lot of the letters in our alphabet came first from Greek, then from Latin, and finally into English.

Some letters of the alphabet have an interesting history. The word **alphabet** is made up of the first two letters of the Greek alphabet. These letters are **alpha** (A, α) and **beta** (B, β). You can hear them in the word **alphabet.**

A letter that has an interesting history is **c.** The Greeks did not have a letter **c.** Neither did the Romans. The Romans had a letter for the **g** sound that looked like this: G, g. They changed it to look like this for the **k** sound: C, c.

The letter **c** makes two sounds in English—the sound like an **s** (as in **cell**) and the sound like **k** (as in **cup**). Since English already has a symbol for the **k** sound (k) and a symbol for the **s** sound (s), we really don't need the symbol **c.** But this symbol is very important to our spelling. Here is why: Some morphographs are pronounced in different ways when they are combined with other morphographs. However, the morphographs are always spelled the same way. The letter **c** can stand for the **s** sound or the **k** sound. So we can spell words like **medic** and **medicine** with the same spelling. If we didn't have the letter **c,** we would have to spell the words this way: **medik, medisine.**

So this is how we got our ABCs. Our **A** and **B** came from Greek, and our **C** came from the Romans.

Below are the letters from the Greek alphabet. After each number write the English letter.
Here's a hint: **Lambda** is **l,** and **Mu** is **m.** You can figure out the letters by looking at them.

Λ, λ (lambda) = l   M, μ (mu) = m

1. O, o (omicron) = _O_

2. T, τ (tau) = _T_

3. B, β (beta) = _b_

4. E, ε (epsilon) = _E_

5. A, α (alpha) = _A_

Answer the items.

6. From what words did the word **alphabet** come? _alpha, beta_

7. Did the letter **c** come from Greek or Latin? _romans_

8. What sound does the **c** in **physic** make when you add **ist?** _"k"_

9. What sound does the **c** in **physic** make when you add **al?** _"k"_

10. What sound does the first **c** in **criticize** make? _"k"_

11. What sound does the second **c** in **criticize** make? _"k"_

12. What are the morphographs in **criticize?** _criti + size_

> Lesson 10 is a test lesson.
> There is no worksheet.

Lesson 11

A

1. _____

2. _____

B

revision   thorough   through   embarrassed   infection

C

Make nine real words from the morphographs in the box.

ly	er	sore	strange	est	ness	sad

1. *strangely*
2. *strangest*
3. *sadness*
4. *sadly*
5. *saddest*
6. *strangest*
7. *sorest*
8. *stranger*
9. *highest*

D

Circle all the words that end in a consonant and the letter **y.**

1. (study)
2. play
3. toy
4. (marry)
5. enjoy
6. spray
7. (cry)
8. (happy)
9. they
10. (pity)
11. relay
12. (nasty)

Write the correct spelling for each word. Then write one of these letters after each word:

Write **O** if the word is spelled by just putting the morphographs together.
Write **A** if the final-**e** rule explains why the spelling is changed.
Write **B** if the doubling rule explains why the spelling is changed.

	word	**rule**
1. ship + ing =	shipping	B
2. race + ing =	racing	A
3. hope + less =	hopeless	O
4. hope + ful =	hopeful	O
5. star + less =	starless	O
6. run + er =	runner	B
7. re + fine + ing =	refining	A
8. verse + ion =	version	A

Write the morphographs for each word. Figure out any morphographs you don't know. Use Word Parts.

1. im + part + ial = impartial

2. fail + ure = failure

3. ac + know + ledge = acknowledge

4. just + ice = justice

Lesson 12

A

1. play + ful = *playful*
2. pity + ful = *pityful*
3. try + ed = *tried*
4. try + ing = *trying*
5. toy + s = *toys*

6. study + ing = *studying*
7. vary + ed = *varied*
8. glory + ous = *glorious*
9. heavy + est = *heavyest*
10. joy + ous = *joyous*

B

1. _____
2. _____
3. _____
4. _____
5. _____
6. _____
7. _____
8. _____

9. _____
10. _____
11. _____
12. _____
13. _____
14. _____
15. _____

C

Add the morphographs together. Remember to use your spelling rules. The morphograph **y** is a vowel letter.

1. fat + y = *fatty*
2. blame + less = *blameless*
3. in + cure + able = *incureable*
4. ease + y = *easy*
5. mis + take + en = *mistaken*

6. run + y = *runny*
7. hope + ful = *hopeful*
8. im + prove + ed = *improved*
9. store + age = *storage*
10. shine + y = *shiny*

D

Write the correct spelling for each word. Then write one of these letters after each word:

Write **O** if the word is spelled by just putting the morphographs together.
Write **A** if the final-**e** rule explains why the spelling is changed.
Write **B** if the doubling rule explains why the spelling is changed.

		word	rule
1.	care + less =	careless	O
2.	fate + al =	fatal	A
3.	plan + ing =	planning	B
4.	move + ment =	movement	O
5.	slam + ed =	slammed	B
6.	judge + ing =	judging	A
7.	shop + er =	shopper	B
8.	mad + ness =	madness	O

E

Make nine real words from the morphographs in the box.

ing	bag	store	age	ed	leak	pack

1. baggage
2. storage
3. storing
4. leaking
5. leakage
6. leaked
7. aged
8. age
9. package

Lesson 13

_____

_____

B

1. stay + ing   = _staying_
2. hurry + ing   = _hurrying_
3. fancy + est   = _fanciest_
4. worry + ed   = _worried_
5. enjoy + ment   = _enjoyment_
6. beauty + ful   = _beautiful_
7. cry + ing   = _crying_
8. say + ing   = _saying_

C

We use paragraphs to show when writing goes from one topic to another. People didn't always use paragraphs, however. The Greeks who wrote over two thousand years ago completely covered the page with writing. There were no spaces between the lines, no commas, and no periods. When they switched topics, they wouldn't indent and start a new paragraph. They made a small mark next to that line. They called this mark a **paragraph.**

The word **paragraph** is made up of two morphographs—**para** and **graph. Para** means "next to." **Graph** means "something written."

Today we usually indent the first line of a new topic instead of writing a little mark beside it. But sometimes we show a new paragraph by skipping a line so that extra space is created between topics. The word **paragraph** is still with us to refer to a change in topic.

1. Name three ways the early Greek writing was different from ours. _They covered the whole page, no indents, they mark a new paragraph._

2. What does the morphograph **para** mean? _next to_

3. What does the morphograph **graph** mean? _something written_

4. How did Greek writers show a change of topic? _a mark_

5. How do we show a change of topic today? _an indent or space_

D

Write the morphographs for each word. Figure out any morphographs you don't know.
Use Word Parts.

1. ___un___ + ___us___ + ual + ___ly___ = unusually

2. ___dis___ + ___eas___ + ed = diseased

3. manu + ___fact___ + ___ure___ = manufacture

4. ___ad___ + ___miss___ + ion = admission

E

A student wrote this report. The report contains seven misspelled words.
Write each of those words correctly.

Many experts agree that spelling is an importent
skill for students to have. If a student mispells words
in a written report, peopel reading the report tend
to judge that the report is poor, even if the content
of the report is excellent and is presented well. Sum
geografy teachers have been known to fail students
for poor spelling. Many teachers do not fail students
but reqire correct spelling on all reportes.

___important___

___misspells___

___people___

___some___

___geography___

___require___

___reports___

Write the correct spelling for each word. Then write one of these letters after each word:

Write **O** if the word is spelled by just putting the morphographs together.
Write **A** if the final-**e** rule explains why the spelling is changed.
Write **B** if the doubling rule explains why the spelling is changed.

		word	rule
1. friend + ly	=	friendly	O
2. please + ure	=	pleasure	O
3. step + ed	=	stepped	B
4. ap + pear + ance	=	appearance	O
5. fort + une + ate	=	fortunate	A
6. skin + y	=	skinny	B

Lesson 14

A

_____

_____

B

visitor   television   devise   bury   deny

C

1. _____   4. _____

2. _____   5. _____

3. _____

D

The morphograph **vise** usually means "to see." Below are some words that use the morphograph **vise.**

visit: When you go to see friends or relatives, you visit them.

supervisor: Someone who is responsible for watching over the work of others is a supervisor.

visible: A visible thing is something you can see.

advise: When you help people solve a problem, you advise them. You help them see the problem more clearly.

television: Tele means "distance." A television permits us to see pictures sent over long distances.

revise: When you revise something you have written, you change it to make it better by seeing it again.

Write the morphographs for each word.

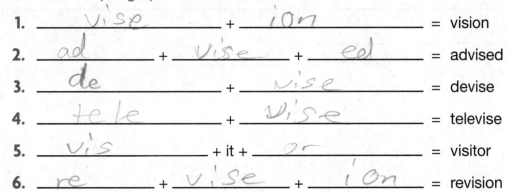

1. ____vise____ + ____ion____ = vision
2. ____ad____ + ____vise____ + ____ed____ = advised
3. ____de____ + ____vise____ = devise
4. ____tele____ + ____vise____ = televise
5. ____vis____ + it + ____or____ = visitor
6. ____re____ + ____vise____ + ____ion____ = revision

Answer these items.

7. Something that is not visible is **invisible.** What does the morphograph **in** mean in this word? _not_

8. A visitor is one who visits you. A supervisor is one who supervises you. What does the morphograph **or** mean? _to do_

Write the correct words containing **vise.**

9. Mrs. McAllister is working on the second _revise_ of the cookbook she is writing.

10. Freddy needs new contact lenses because his _vision_ is poor.

11. Marsha _advised_ me to begin my book report right away.

12. I wonder if any network is going to _televise_ the world soccer championships.

E

Make seven real words from the morphographs in the box.

mis	en	hap	take	s

1. _mistaken_
2. _happy_
3. _takes_
4. _misspell_
5. _happen_
6. _taken_
7. _happyness_

Add the morphographs together. Remember to use your spelling rules.

1. play + ful = _playful_
2. sturdy + est = _sturdiest_
3. marry + ed = _married_
4. deny + al = _denial_
5. copy + ed = _coppied_
6. hap + y + ness = _happyness_
7. carry + age = _carrage_
8. bury + ed = _burried_
9. dry + ing = _drying_
10. try + al = _trial_

Lesson 15 is a test lesson.
There is no worksheet.

Lesson 16

A

B

Three of these words are misspelled. Use Word Parts to find the correct spellings. Write the misspelled words correctly.

1. embarassed   _____
2. paragraph
3. revision   _____
4. easiest
5. burial   _____
6. thorough
7. visitor
8. appeer
9. critisize

C

Write the morphographs for each word. Figure out any morphographs you don't know. Use Word Parts.

1. _____ + _____ + ary = imaginary

2. _____ + _____ + _____ + _____ = informative

3. _____ + _____ + ant = unpleasant

4. _____ + _____ = paragraph

D

Add the morphographs together. Remember to use your spelling rules. The morphograph **y** is a vowel letter.

1. noise + y + er   = _____
2. com + mit + ment = _____
3. hap + en   = _____
4. busy + ness   = _____
5. en + joy + ed   = _____
6. per + hap + s   = _____
7. use + ual   = _____
8. in + vise + ible = _____
9. strange + ly   = _____
10. o + mit   = _____
11. hap + y + ly   = _____
12. super + vise + ion = _____

E

Write the word for each meaning clue.

visible   advise   supervisor

1. someone who is responsible for watching over the work of others   _____
2. can be seen   _____
3. to help someone solve a problem   _____

Lesson 17

A

1. _____

2. _____

B

Make twelve real words from the morphographs in the box. The letter **x** acts like two consonant letters.

y	sun	wax	luck	wit	er	hap	est

1. _____   7. _____

2. _____   8. _____

3. _____   9. _____

4. _____   10. _____

5. _____   11. _____

6. _____   12. _____

C

Write the correct spelling for each word. Then write one of these letters after each word:

Write **O** if the word is spelled by just putting the morphographs together.
Write **A** if the final-**e** rule explains why the spelling is changed.
Write **B** if the doubling rule explains why the spelling is changed.
Write **C** if the **y**-to-**i** rule explains why the spelling is changed.

	word	**rule**
1. hazard + ous	= _____	_____
2. hap + en	= _____	_____
3. athlete + ic + s	= _____	_____
4. bury + al	= _____	_____

	word	rule

5. re + place + ment = _____ _____

6. hurry + ing   = _____ _____

7. swim + er   = _____ _____

8. in + quire + ed   = _____ _____

D

Some morphographs have more than one meaning. The morphograph **sent** has three different meanings.

One meaning of **sent** is "to send in the past": We sent the package yesterday. We will send another one tomorrow.

Another meaning of **sent** is "to feel." The word **consent** has this meaning. When you **consent** to something, you feel that it is all right to do. The words re**sent,** dis**sent,** and **sent**imental also have the meaning "to feel."

Another meaning of **sent** is "to exist." The morphograph **ab** means "away." When you are absent, you are not here. You exist away from here. The opposite of **absent** is **present.** **Pre** means "in front of." When you are present, you are in front of us.

Match the correct meaning of **sent** for each underlined word.

      feeling   exist   send in the past

1. I <u>resent</u> her coming here.   _____

2. Acme Company <u>sent</u> us the bill last week.   _____

3. Susie was <u>present</u> at the meeting.   _____

4. He is very <u>sentimental</u> about his past.   _____

5. My mother never <u>consents</u> to letting me stay out late. _____

6. Yesterday no one was <u>absent</u> from class.   _____

Lesson 18

A

1. _____
2. _____
3. _____
4. _____

B

Write the correct word for each sentence. If you are not sure of a word, look it up in the list of homonyms on pages 242–245.

1. They made a **right/write** turn.   _____

2. Look over **their/there.**   _____

3. I can't **hear/here** you.   _____

4. I have a **hole/whole** in my stocking.   _____

C

Write the correct spelling for each word. Then write one of these letters after each word:

Write **O** if the word is spelled by just putting the morphographs together.
Write **A** if the final-**e** rule explains why the spelling is changed.
Write **B** if the doubling rule explains why the spelling is changed.
Write **C** if the **y**-to-**i** rule explains why the spelling is changed.

	word	rule
1. stop + ing =	_____	_____
2. deny + ing =	_____	_____
3. please + ant =	_____	_____
4. im + prove + ment =	_____	_____
5. hid + en =	_____	_____
6. worry + some =	_____	_____

D

Add the morphographs together. Remember to use your spelling rules.

1. cry + ing   = _____

2. un + fix + ed   = _____

3. hap + y   = _____

4. embarrass + ment   = _____

5. friend + ly + est = _____

6. per + mit   = _____

7. copy + ing   = _____

8. ac + know + ledge = _____

9. box + er   = _____

10. manu + fact + ure + er = _____

E

Make twelve real words from the morphographs in the box.

bake	shop	s	swim	er	wrap	ing

1. _____   7. _____

2. _____   8. _____

3. _____   9. _____

4. _____   10. _____

5. _____   11. _____

6. _____   12. _____

Lesson 19

A

1. _____   6. _____
2. _____   7. _____
3. _____   8. _____
4. _____   9. _____
5. _____   10. _____

B

Write the correct word for each sentence. If you are not sure of a word, look it up in the list of homonyms on pages 242–245.

1. Shawn can sing the **hole/whole** song.   _____

2. We walked **threw/through** the building.   _____

3. Bill told a very imaginative **tail/tale.**   _____

4. We know how to **sail/sale** a boat.   _____

5. Murry is asking the bank for a **loan/lone.**   _____

6. There is only one **peace/piece** of pie left.   _____

C

A student wrote this report. The report contains eleven misspelled words. Write each of those words correctly. If you're not sure of a contraction, look it up in the list of contractions on page 241.

If you want to be an athlete, you have to work out every day. Swiming and runing are good exercises four improoving you're body. Atheletic activities dont' always reqwire grate phisical strength, but they do reqwire a lot of training.

_____
_____
_____
_____
_____   _____
_____   _____
_____   _____

D

Write the morphographs for each word. Figure out any morphographs you don't know. Use Word Parts.

1. _____ + com + _____ + _____ = accommodate

2. _____ + _____ = dispel

3. _____ + ual = casual

4. _____ + _____ = receive

E

The Greeks were superstitious. They believed that events could be predicted by studying the stars. Their morphographs for **star** are **aster** and **astro.**

The Greek word **astrology** means "the study of stars for predicting future events." An **astrologer** is not a scientist, but someone who tells future events by studying stars.

The scientific study of stars and planets is called **astronomy.** The morphograph **nome** means "to name." An **astronomer** is a scientist who identifies stars and other heavenly bodies. An astronomer can name the stars.

The Greeks thought that a disaster was caused by bad stars. Today we use the word **disaster** to mean "a terrible event."

The word **astronomical** means "extremely large" or "great, like the universe."

Answer the questions. You may use Word Parts.

1. Why do you think this punctuation mark * is called an asterisk? Write the morphographs for **asterisk** with plus signs.

   _____

2. Write the morphographs for **astronomy, astronomical,** and **astronomer.**

   _____

3. Is an **astrologer** a scientist? Is an **astronomer** a scientist? _____

4. The morphograph **naut** means "sailor." The morphograph **cosmo** means "world." Russian space travelers are called **cosmonauts.** The name for space travelers from the United States contains the Greek morphograph for **star.** What's the name?

   _____

5. If something is given the wrong name, it is called a **misnomer.** Write the morphographs

   for **misnomer.** _____

```
Lesson 20 is a test lesson.
There is no worksheet.
```

Lesson 21

A

1. _____

2. _____

3. _____

4. _____

B

Do not use Word Parts for Part B.

In 1613, a Dutch trading ship that was anchored near
Manhattan Island caught fire. Attempts to save the ship
failed, and the crew had to go ashore. Onshore, friendly
Native Americans offered survivors food and shelter.
Encouraged by the warm welcome, the Dutch decided to
build their first colony on that site, which later became
New York City. Who were the first European settlers of
New York City?

    Some Duch traders had to abandon there burning
ship, which was ankered near Manhattan Iland. Some
freindly Native Americans gave food and shelter
to the traders. The traders found the wellcome so
encuraging that they desided to bild a collony, which
became New York City.

_____

_____

_____

_____

_____

_____

_____

_____

_____

_____

C

Write the correct spelling for each word. Then write one of these letters after each word:

Write **O** if the word is spelled by just putting the morphographs together.
Write **A** if the final-**e** rule explains why the spelling is changed.
Write **B** if the doubling rule explains why the spelling is changed.
Write **C** if the **y**-to-**i** rule explains why the spelling is changed.

		word	**rule**
1.	oc + case + ion =	_____	_____
2.	cur + ent =	_____	_____
3.	fant + as + y =	_____	_____
4.	ad + vise + ed =	_____	_____
5.	oc + cur =	_____	_____
6.	deny + ing =	_____	_____
7.	plan + ed =	_____	_____
8.	vary + ous =	_____	_____

D

Some words that contain an **f** sound in our language are spelled with the letters **ph**. These words come from Greek words, not from Latin words or French words. The words gra**ph**, **ph**oto, and s**ph**ere are words that come from Greek.

The reason these words are spelled with **ph** rather than **f** has to do with letters in the Greek alphabet. The symbol used for the **f** sound in the Greek Alphabet is Φ. The name of this symbol is **phi.**

When the Romans translated Greek symbols, they used the letters **ph** to stand for Φ. So words that have **ph** for the **f** sound come from Greek.

1. For each of the words below, write the morphographs that come from Greek. For example, the morphographs in **philosophy** that come from Greek are **philo** and **soph.**

soph + ist + ic + ate + ed	= sophisticated	_____
re + phrase	= rephrase	_____
morpho + graph	= morphograph	_____
physic + al	= physical	_____

2. The word **uphill** does not come from Greek. How do you know it's not Greek even though it has **ph?** _____

_____

3. Sometimes the Romans would change the Greek **ph** spelling to **f.** The Greek morphograph **phant** means "something seen." The word **phantom** has the morphograph **phant.** Two of our English words used to be spelled **phantasy** and **phantastic.** Write the correct modern spelling of these two words that originally came from Greek. _____

_____

4. The morphograph **phet** means "to speak" in the word **prophet.** The morphograph **fess** means "to speak" in the word **confess.** Which morphograph shows Latin spelling, **phet** or **fess?** Which morphograph shows Greek spelling? _____

_____

5. Writing and drawing on walls has been going on for hundreds of years. The Romans called it **graffito.** The plural word for **graffito** is **graffiti.** What Greek morphograph means the same as Roman **graf?** _____

_____

Lesson 22

1. _____
2. _____
3. _____
4. _____

B

Do not use Word Parts for Part B.

Wool was very important to the economy in England four hundred years ago. The king passed a law requiring everyone over the age of seven to wear a wool cap. This law was designed to sell more wool. Anyone who did not comply with the law was fined. Wool was so important to England that anyone selling sheep outside the country was punished by death.

Why were wool caps a common sight in England 400 years ago?

      Because of the econnomic importence of wool in England, the king past a law which recuired everyone to where a wool cap. This happened for hundred years ago. Being seen without one resulted in being find, so nearly everyone complyed with the law.

_____

_____

_____

_____

_____

_____

_____

_____

Write the morphographs for each word. Figure out any morphographs you don't know. Use Word Parts.

1. mode + _____ + _____ = modernize

2. _____ + _____ = another

3. _____ + _____ + _____ = misfortune

4. _____ + _____ + _____ = philosopher

5. _____ + _____ + _____ = consistent

6. _____ + _____ + _____ + ate + _____ = accomodation

7. _____ + _____ = imagine

8. _____ + _____ = poisonous

Write the correct word or words for each sentence. If you're not sure of a word, look it up in the list of homonyms on pages 242–245.

1. A little **peace/piece** and quiet will do her good. _____

2. Cynthia bought some **plain/plane** white paper. _____

3. I wish she **wood/would right/write** to me. _____

4. **Meat/Meet** is **vary/very** expensive these days. _____

Lesson 23

A

By eating pears, he lost weight around his waist.

B

Add the morphographs together. Remember to use your spelling rules.

1. cur + ent = _____
2. oc + case + ion + al + ly = _____
3. astro + nome + er = _____
4. com + mode + ity = _____
5. fant + as + y + es = _____
6. dure + ing = _____
7. re + phrase + ed = _____
8. ap + ply + ed = _____
9. hemi + sphere = _____
10. case + ual + ty = _____

C

Write the correct word for each sentence. If you're not sure of a word, look it up in the list of homonyms on pages 242–245.

1. Sally is learning how to fly a **plain/plane.** _____
2. **Where/Wear** are you going? _____
3. The dog chased its **tail/tale.** _____
4. The deer fled **threw/through** the forest. _____

A student wrote this report. Seven words are misspelled. Write each of those words correctly.

We viseted a great, beautyful hotel last summer. This hotel was a fashionable resort for people who like to go swimming and play tennis. The hotel was origenally built in 1890, but the acomodations were comfortable and moderne. We were required to wear formel clothes for the evening meal, but we didn't mind. It was fun. Unfortunatly, we made reservations for only two nights. I wish we could have stayed longer.

_____

_____

_____

_____

_____

_____

_____

Lesson 24

A

1. _____ 11. _____
2. _____ 12. _____
3. _____ 13. _____
4. _____ 14. _____
5. _____ 15. _____
6. _____ 16. _____
7. _____ 17. _____
8. _____ 18. _____
9. _____ 19. _____
10. _____ 20. _____

B

Write the correct spelling for each word. Then write one of these letters after each word:

Write **O** if the word is spelled by just putting the morphographs together.
Write **A** if the final-**e** rule explains why the spelling is changed.
Write **B** if the doubling rule explains why the spelling is changed.
Write **C** if the **y**-to-**i** rule explains why the spelling is changed.

	word	rule
1. act + ual + ly	= _____	_____
2. knot + ed	= _____	_____
3. like + ly + hood	= _____	_____
4. verse + ion	= _____	_____
5. in + con + sist + ent	= _____	_____
6. en + dure + ance	= _____	_____
7. com + ply + ing	= _____	_____
8. step + ing	= _____	_____
9. mode + er + ate	= _____	_____
10. fun + y	= _____	_____

Write the correct word for each sentence. If you're not sure of a word, look it up in the list of homonyms on pages 242–245.

1. I'm hoping that the **weather/whether** will change. _____

2. He performed a daring **feat/feet**. _____

3. We will **meat/meet** in another room. _____

4. Where **wood/would** you like to sit? _____

Find the misspelled words in the student's answer. Then write them correctly.
Do not use Word Parts.

For years, industry emptied chemical waste of all types into the Cuyahoga River, which winds through Cleveland, Ohio, in the United States. Cleveland's residents occasionally complained about the river's vile condition, but nothing was done about it until 1969. In that year, the thick, oily surface of the river, littered with trash and rubble, caught fire, and the fire would not go out. The poisonous waterway blazed for days. The fire destroyed warehouses and factories along the riverbank. Finally the embarrassed community of Cleveland decided to clean up the Cuyahoga.

What stopped the polluting of the Cuyahoga River? _____

    Factries dumped chemikals into the river.
This industreal waist combined with litter, and
the hole river caught fire. The fire distroyed
wherehouses and embarassed the city's
recidents.

_____   _____   _____

_____   _____   _____

Lesson 25 is a test lesson.
There is no worksheet.

Lesson 26

A _____

_____

B _____

_____

C _____

As you know, many words in English came first from Greek, then Latin, then French and finally came into English. For many of these words, the spelling changed each time the word went into a new language.

Some words did not follow these steps. Instead they went from Latin directly into English. Here's why they didn't go from Latin to French and then to English:

Two thousand years ago, a great Roman general named Julius Caesar led an army that invaded England. The Roman invaders spoke Latin. The English used some Latin words to communicate with the invaders. These words went directly from Latin into English.

For hundreds of years, people who were well educated learned to read Latin. Some Latin words became part of the English language.

Below are some words that went directly from Latin into English. Notice that the spellings changed.

Latin	English
tributum	tribute
milites (soldiers)	military, militant
discipulus	disciple
credo	creed
victoria	victory
fortuna	fortune
planta	plant

Write the answers to the items.

1. Many words in English came from Greek, then Latin, then French. Did the word **fortune** follow these steps? How did the Romans spell the word **fortune?**

   _____

2. Why did people who spoke English 2,000 years ago learn some Latin words?

   _____

Use English words from the list to complete each item.

3. The entire school was excited about the team's _____.

4. His success was due to good _____.

5. The Garden Shop sells hundreds of _____.

6. The word **discipline** is related to the word _____.

D

Five of these words are misspelled. Find the misspelled words. Then write them correctly.

1. importance   _____
2. acommodate
3. beautiful   _____
4. desaster
5. thorough   _____
6. omit
7. refrase   _____
8. embarrassed
9. consistent   _____
10. ocur
11. indurance
12. casually

E

Write the morphographs for each word. Figure out any morphographs you don't know. Use Word Parts.

1. _____ + _____ = military

2. dis + _____ + _____ = discipline

3. _____ + _____ = begin

4. _____ + ate + _____ = duration

Lesson 27

A

B

| origin | disaster | graphic | invisible | astronomer | advise |

Write the word for each meaning clue.

1. a drawing   _____

2. where something comes from   _____

3. can't be seen   _____

4. a scientist who can name the stars   _____

5. a terrible event   _____

6. to help someone solve a problem   _____

C

Circle the misspelled word in each group. Then write it correctly.

1. medicine
   prehaps
   acknowledge
   valuable
   _____

2. shopper
   athletically
   intrest
   separate
   _____

3. suported
   usage
   autobiography
   easier
   _____

4. admirable
   information
   pulsate
   mistriel
   _____

5. performance
   confusion
   flatten
   freindliness
   _____

6. imaginary
   plesure
   basic
   service
   _____

Add the morphographs together. Remember to use your spelling rules. **W** at the end of a morphograph is a vowel letter.

1. trans + fer   = _____

2. know + ledge   = _____

3. pro + pel   = _____

4. al + lot + ment   = _____

5. com + mit + ment = _____

6. grow + th   = _____

7. hap + y + est   = _____

8. vise + ual   = _____

9. al + low + ed   = _____

10. industry + al   = _____

Lesson 28

B

---

1. pro + pel + ing   = _____

2. ad + mit + ance   = _____

3. com + mit + ment = _____

4. re + cur + ing   = _____

5. trans + fer + ed   = _____

6. cur + tail   = _____

7. al + lot + ed   = _____

8. ex + cel + ence   = _____

9. for + got + en   = _____

10. un + hap + y   = _____

C

When **ch** sounds like **k** in a word, it probably came from Greek. Here is why. The Greeks had two different sounds for **k.** One sounded like our **k** sound. The other Greek **k** sound sounded like a hoarse **k.** The Romans did not have a letter for this sound, so they used their letters **c** and **h** to write this sound: **ch.**

Here are some words that had this letter in Greek: **ch**emical, s**ch**ool, me**ch**anic, and stoma**ch**.

People often misspell words that have this **ch** spelling for the **k** sound. Here are some words that are often misspelled: psy**ch**ology, **ch**aracter, heada**ch**e, melan**ch**oly, me**ch**anics, te**ch**nique.

Write the answers to the items.

1. How many **k** sounds did the Greeks have?   _____

2. How do you know the word **scheme** comes from Greek?   _____

3. Does the word **change** come from Greek? How do you know?   _____

4. Does the word **echo** come from Greek? How do you know?   _____

5. Two Roman letters aren't pronounced in the word **psychology.** Which letters are they?   _____

Add the morphographs together. Use your rules. All these words have the **k** sound spelled **ch**.

6. school + ing = _____

7. character + ist + ic = _____

8. head + ache = _____

9. mechan + ic + al = _____

10. cheme + ist + ry = _____

11. echo + es = _____

12. back + ache = _____

13. cheme + ic + al = _____

14. scheme + ate + ic = _____

15. anchor + ed = _____

16. melan + choly = _____

17. chore + us = _____

18. chord + s = _____

19. techno + loge + y = _____

D

Make eight real words from the morphographs in the box.

en	bid	for	sake	give	got

1. _____ 5. _____

2. _____ 6. _____

3. _____ 7. _____

4. _____ 8. _____

E

Write the morphographs for each word. Figure out any morphographs you don't know. Use Word Parts.

1. _____ + th + _____ = healthy

2. _____ + trol + _____ = controlled

3. _____ + _____ = safety

4. _____ + gin + _____ = beginning

Lesson 29

A

1. _____

2. _____

B

1. o + mit + ed = _____

2. oc + cur + ence = _____

3. al + lot + ment = _____

4. per + mit + ing = _____

5. pro + pel + er = _____

6. pre + fer + ed = _____

7. com + mit + ee = _____

8. per + hap + s = _____

9. ex + cel + ed = _____

10. un + con + trol + able = _____

11. re + pel + ent = _____

C

Write the correct word for each sentence. If you are not sure of a word, look it up in the list of homonyms on pages 242–245.

1. Please come **hear/here.** _____

2. The book has a **plain/plane** cover. _____

3. **Their/They're** answers were all **right/write.** _____

4. Our house is for **sail/sale.** _____

D

Five words are misspelled. Find the misspelled words. Then write them correctly.

1. confuseing   _____
2. consistent
3. transfir   _____
4. skeme
5. fantazy   _____
6. knowledge
7. industrial   _____
8. safety
9. excelent   _____

E

Add the morphographs together. Remember to use your spelling rules.

1. character + ist + ic = _____

2. image + ine + ary   = _____

3. mechan + ism   = _____

4. cheme + ic + al   = _____

5. marry + age   = _____

6. mode + est + y   = _____

7. lone + ly + ness   = _____

8. be + gin + er   = _____

F

In Lesson 31 you'll have a spelling contest. Some of the words below will be used in the contest.

physical	current	permission	character	carriage
physicist	poison	inform	philosophy	improvement
athlete	usual	modern	endurance	appearance

Lesson 30 is a test lesson.
There is no worksheet.

Lesson 31

personal   personnel   questionable   questionnaire   personify   personality

B

1. _____

2. _____

C

English borrowed many words from French. Sometimes we used the French spelling. Other times we changed the spelling. Hundreds of years ago, the French word **personne** was taken over by the English. In England its spelling was changed to **person.** The morphograph **person** can be found in many words like **person**ify, **person**al, and **person**ality. Later, English borrowed another word from French: **personnel.** The word **personnel** means "a group of workers." The English word **personnel** was not built on the English morphograph **person;** it was borrowed directly from French and has kept the French spelling. This is why **personnel** is not like all the other words with **person. Personnel** has the French spelling with two **n**'s.

The French word **questionne** had a similar history. When we borrowed it, we changed the spelling to **question** and built many common words with it, like **question**able and un**question**ing. Much later, we borrowed the word **questionnaire.** We took the word **questionnaire** directly from the French instead of building a new word from our word **question.** So **questionnaire** has kept the original French spelling with two **n**'s.

Here are some regular English words. Write the morphographs for each word.

1. _____ + _____ + _____ = impersonal

2. quest + _____ = question

3. _____ + _____ + _____ = impersonate

4. _____ + _____ + _____ = personalize

5. _____ + _____ = personify

6. _____ + _____ + _____ + _____ = unquestionable

7. _____ + _____ + ity = personality

Write the answer for each item.

8. Why is **personnel** spelled with two **n**'s?   _____

9. Is the word **personal** based on French or English spelling?   _____

10. Is **person** a short **cvc** morphograph? So in the word **person + ify,** does the **n** double?   _____

D

Find the misspelled words in the sentences. Then write the words correctly.

1. Only very important people were admited.   _____

2. His autobiagraphy is excellent.   _____

3. They misplased their bagage at the airport.   _____

4. It was definitly a joyus ocasion.   _____

E

Three words in this exercise have the morphograph **duce** or the morphograph **duct.** In Latin **duce** and **duct** mean "to lead." Something that is conducted is led together. Add the morphographs together.

1. pro + duct + ion   = _____

2. dis + ciple + ine + ary = _____

3. re + duce + ed   = _____

4. re + cur + ent   = _____

5. con + duct + or   = _____

6. sur + round + ing   = _____

7. re + bel + ion   = _____

8. busy + ness + es   = _____

9. dure + ing   = _____

10. e + duce + ate   = _____

Lesson 32

On that site, she received a citation.

1. _____

2. _____

Find the misspelled words in the student's answer. Then write the words correctly. Do not use Word Parts for this part.

Years ago, a group of farmers in central California decided that they had a coyote problem. They trapped, shot, and poisoned the coyotes until almost none remained. With all the coyotes gone, the number of mice skyrocketed until there were over 80,000 per acre. The mice overran the land, destroying millions of dollars worth of crops. Now the farmers really had a problem!

Why did the farmers decide to stop killing coyotes?   _____

The farmers probibly desided to stop traping   _____
and poizoning the coyotes because the coyotes
are helpfull in killing the mice. The mice are a reel   _____
problem now, and the farmers wish the coyotes
were back.   _____

_____   _____

Write the correct spelling for each word. Then write one of these letters after each word:

Write **O** if the word is spelled by just putting the morphographs together.
Write **A** if the final-**e** rule explains why the spelling is changed.
Write **B** if the doubling rule explains why the spelling is changed.
Write **C** if the **y**-to-**i** rule explains why the spelling is changed.

	word	rule
1. mechan + ism	= _____	_____
2. oc + cur + ed	= _____	_____
3. family + ar	= _____	_____
4. con + trol + ing	= _____	_____
5. re + com + mend + ed	= _____	_____
6. probe + able	= _____	_____
7. re + ceive + er	= _____	_____
8. manu + script	= _____	_____

56 Lesson 32

© SRA/McGraw-Hill. All rights reserved.

The Greeks used **y** as a vowel more than we do. The Greeks had many words with **y** between two consonants. Some words borrowed from Greek are still spelled this way. In fact, most of our words that have **y** between two consonants came from Greek. The **y** in these words is a vowel letter. Here are some of those words: s**y**mbol, c**y**cle, m**y**stery, ps**y**cholog**y**, anal**y**sis, h**y**steria, rh**y**thm, ph**y**sical, paral**y**zed, s**y**non**y**mous, t**y**rant, h**y**pocrite, h**y**phen, ox**y**gen, h**y**pnosis, h**y**mn, h**y**drant.

Answer the items.

1. How do you know the word **hymn** comes from Greek?

   _____

2. Does the word **symbol** come from Greek? How do you know?

   _____

Add the morphographs together.

3. myst + ic + al   = _____

4. syn + onym   = _____

5. physic + ian   = _____

6. syn + onym + ous   = _____

7. hymn + al   = _____

8. hyphen + ate + ed   = _____

9. symbol + ic   = _____

10. myst + er + y + ous = _____

11. bi + cycle   = _____

12. rhythm + ic + al   = _____

13. an + onym + ous   = _____

14. hyster + ic + al   = _____

Lesson 33

A

1. _____ 4. _____

2. _____ 5. _____

3. _____ 6. _____

B

Circle the misspelled word in each group. Then write it correctly.

1. present
   exercise
   lengthy
   misterious

   _____

2. embarrass
   approach
   thoughtfull
   personnel

   _____

3. wonderful
   actually
   durring
   echo

   _____

4. intermission
   personality
   questionned
   symbolic

   _____

5. excellance
   computer
   enlighten
   autograph

   _____

6. manufacture
   inconsistent
   surround
   advize

   _____

C

Write the morphographs for each word.

1. _____ + _____ + _____ = disappoint

2. _____ + onym = synonym

3. _____ + _____ = magician

4. _____ + _____ = fourth

5. _____ + _____ + _____ + _____ = unforgettable

6. _____ + _____ + _____ = regrettable

D

The morphograph **dict** means "speak" or "speech." Here are some words that use the morphograph **dict**.

dictate: You dictate when you give instructions out loud.

predict: The morphograph **pre** means "before." You predict something when you tell about it before it happens.

diction: The way you use words is your diction.

contradict: The morphograph **contra** means "opposite." When you say the opposite of what someone else has said, you contradict that person.

Write the morphographs for each word.

1. _____ + _____ = diction

2. _____ + _____ + _____ = prediction

3. _____ + _____ = contradict

4. _____ + _____ + _____ = dictation

Answer the items.

5. What does the morphograph **contra** mean? _____

6. What does the morphograph **pre** mean? _____

Write the correct words that contain **dict**.

7. The way she uses words is impressive. I wish I had her _____

8. I went to a friend who said he could _____ where I would be next week.

9. Fred always thinks the opposite of his sister. That's why he often _____ the things she says.

10. Mr. Martinez said, "Write **Part B** on your paper. I'm going to _____ some spelling words to you."

11. Some people can _____ the weather just by looking at the clouds.

Lesson 34

A

indict   edict   malediction   benediction

B

_____

C

1. _____

2. _____

D

Find the misspelled words in these sentences. Then write the words correctly.

1. They aproached the campground with happyness.   _____

2. Some poisenous animals were in the area.   _____

3. They were not permited to camp near the lake.   _____

4. My philosephy is actally very realistic.   _____

5. Four road hazzards led to much confuseion.   _____

E

Make ten real words from the morphographs in the box.

cur	oc	ence	s	re	ed	con

1. _____   6. _____

2. _____   7. _____

3. _____   8. _____

4. _____   9. _____

5. _____   10. _____

60 Lesson 34

© SRA/McGraw-Hill. All rights reserved.

In Lesson 33 you learned that the morphograph **dict** means "speech" or "speak." Here are other words that contain **dict**.

benediction: A benediction is speaking well of or a blessing.

malediction: A malediction is speaking badly about or a curse.

dictionary: A dictionary is an alphabetical listing of words with their pronunciations and meanings.

dictator: A dictator is a person who tells others what to do or has absolute power.

edict: An edict is an order or command.

indict: To indict is to charge with a crime in a court of law.

Write the morphographs for each word.

1. _____ + _____ = predict

2. _____ + _____ + _____ = dictator

3. _____ + _____ + _____ = malediction

4. _____ + _____ + _____ = dictionary

5. _____ + _____ = edict

6. _____ + _____ + _____ = contradiction

7. _____ + _____ + _____ = indictment

8. _____ + _____ + _____ = benediction

Write the correct words that contain the morphograph **dict.**

9. When I don't know the meaning of a word, I use the _____.

10. The captain runs his ship as if he were a _____.

11. The speaker closed the service with a _____.

12. The peasants were unhappy when they learned about the king's newest

    _____.

13. First he said one thing; then he said the opposite. He always _____ himself.

14. After studying the evidence for several weeks, the city attorney _____ two city officials.

> Lesson 35 is a test lesson.
> There is no worksheet.

Lesson 36

A

1. _____

2. _____

3. _____

4. _____

B

The morphograph **sum** means "the highest or topmost." When Greeks and Romans counted or worked addition problems, they didn't start at the top and write their answer at the bottom. They started at the bottom and worked upwards, writing the total at the top. They called the total the sum because it was the topmost number.

When you give a **summary,** you tell a condensed version of something larger. You tell only about things of the highest importance.

The word **summit** means "the top or highest part." The summit of a mountain is the top of the mountain.

Write the morphographs for each word.

1. _____ + ar + _____ = summary

2. _____ + it = summit

3. _____ + _____ + _____ = summarize

4. _____ + _____ = sums

5. _____ + _____ + _____ + _____ + _____ = summarization

6. _____ + ate + _____ = summation

7. _____ + _____ = summed

C

Write the word for each meaning clue.

dictionary   consent   support   dictate

personnel   indict   contradict   absent

1. a group of workers _____

2. hold something up _____

3. when you are not here _____

4. a book for finding word meanings _____

5. say the opposite of what someone else has said _____

6. feel that something is all right _____

7. say words for someone to write _____

8. when the court tells you that you have done something against the law _____

D

Write the morphographs for each word.

1. _____ + _____ + _____ = indictment

2. _____ + _____ + _____ = separate

3. _____ + _____ = symbolic

4. _____ + er + _____ = mystery

5. _____ + _____ + _____ + _____ = discoveries

6. _____ + _____ + _____ + _____ = characterization

7. _____ + _____ + _____ = synonymous

8. _____ + _____ + _____ = transferred

9. _____ + _____ + _____ = deceived

10. _____ + _____ = perceive

Lesson 37

A

1. _____   11. _____

2. _____   12. _____

3. _____   13. _____

4. _____   14. _____

5. _____   15. _____

6. _____   16. _____

7. _____   17. _____

8. _____   18. _____

9. _____   19. _____

10. _____   20. _____

B

The morphograph for the number **4** is usually **four.** This morphograph is used in **fourteen** and other words. Another morphograph is used for **4** in the words **forty** and **forties.**

Here are words with the morphographs **for** and **four.** Notice that you use a hyphen in words like **forty-one.**

forty	forties	four	four hundred two
fortieth	two hundred forty	ninety-four	fourteenth
forty-one	nineteen forties	forth	three hundred thirty-four

Write these numbers below. Then write the word for each number.

Example: 40s = forties

400 = _____   94th = _____

140 = _____   40th = _____

14 = _____   4th = _____

Write the morphographs for these words. Some morphographs are given.

1. _____ + th = fourth

2. _____ + _____ = fourteen

3. _____ + ty = forty

64 Lesson 37

4. _____ + _____ + es = forties

5. _____ + _____ + _____ = fourteenth

6. _____ + _____ + eth = fortieth

C

Write the correct spelling for each word. Then write one of these letters after each word:

Write **O** if the word is spelled by just putting the morphographs together.
Write **A** if the final-**e** rule explains why the spelling is changed.
Write **B** if the doubling rule explains why the spelling is changed.
Write **C** if the **y**-to-**i** rule explains why the spelling is changed.

		word	rule
1.	early + er	= _____	_____
2.	re + ject + ion	= _____	_____
3.	re + bel + s	= _____	_____
4.	ac + know + ledge + ed	= _____	_____
5.	be + gin + ing	= _____	_____
6.	sum + ar + ize	= _____	_____
7.	com + pel + ed	= _____	_____
8.	pre + dict +able	= _____	_____

D

We're going to treat **i-t-y** as one morphograph even though it's actually two morphographs. **Ity** is made by combining **i-t-e** plus **y** or combining **i-t** plus **y.** In either case, we end up with **i-t-y.** So we'll just treat **ity** as if it is one morphograph.

Add the morphographs together.

1. person + al + ity = _____

2. com + mode + ity = _____

3. dense + ity = _____

4. op + port + une + ity = _____

Lesson 38

There was a large hole in the beam, which made the bridge weak.

B

1. _____

2. _____

C

Add **ance** and **ing** to the words in the box to make twelve real words. Use your spelling rules.

admit	perform	endure	vary	import	appear

1. _____   7. _____

2. _____   8. _____

3. _____   9. _____

4. _____   10. _____

5. _____   11. _____

6. _____   12. _____

D

Write the morphographs for each word.

1. _____ + _____ + _____ = recommend

2. _____ + _____ = various

3. _____ + nox = equinox

4. _____ + _____ + _____ = fortieth

5. _____ + _____ + _____ = activity

6. _____ + _____ = summed

7. _____ + vale + _____ = equivalent

8. _____ + _____ + _____ = preferring

Sometimes words that are related have morphographs that have slightly different spellings. The morphographs **four** and **for** are called **allomorphs.** Another pair of allomorphs is **scribe** and **script.** The morphograph **scribe** means "to write," and it is used in these words: de**scribe,** in**scribe.** The words de**script**ion, in**script**ion, and **scrip**ture also contain a morphograph that means "to write." The morphograph is **script.**

Sometimes an allomorph makes a word easier to pronounce. The word **prescription** is much easier to pronounce than it would be with the allomorph **scribe.**

Write the morphographs for each word.

1. _____ + _____ = subscribe

2. _____ + _____ + _____ = subscription

3. _____ + _____ + _____ + _____ = indescribable

4. _____ + _____ = manuscript

5. _____ + _____ = prescribe

6. _____ + _____ + _____ = prescription

Answer the items.

7. What do you call morphographs that have the same meaning but slightly different spellings? _____

8. Look at these words: **admission/admit, permissible/permit, submissive/submit.** Write the allomorph for **miss.** _____

9. Write the allomorph for **scribe.** _____

Lesson 39

A

find   fury   create   close   story   list

B

1. _____   4. _____

2. _____   5. _____

3. _____   6. _____

C

A student wrote this report. The report contains nine misspelled words. Write each of those words correctly.

     Elephants are dissappearing rapidly. Unfortunetly,
people kill them for there ivory tusks. Ivory is
valueable not only because it is beutiful, but because
it is used as a currancy like gold and silver coins in
some countries. Its really regretable that these
wonderfull creatures are being killed.

_____

_____

_____

_____

_____   _____   _____

_____   _____

D

For words that have the morphograph **ceive,** there are related words that have the allomorph **cept.** When the **ceive** word ends in **ion** or **ive,** the allomorph **cept** is used.

Here are words that have the allomorph **ceive:**

     conceivable   deceive   perceive   misconceive   receive

Here are related words that end in **ion** or **ive:**

     conception   deceptive   perception   misconception   receptive

For each word with **ceive,** write a real word that ends with **ion** or **ive.**

1. misconceive   _____

2. receive   _____

3. perceive   _____

4. preconceived   _____

5. deceive   _____

68   Lesson 39

E

Write the correct spelling for each word. Then write one of these letters after each word:

Write **O** if the word is spelled by just putting the morphographs together.
Write **A** if the final-**e** rule explains why the spelling is changed.
Write **B** if the doubling rule explains why the spelling is changed.
Write **C** if the **y**-to-**i** rule explains why the spelling is changed.

	word	rule
1. sum + ar + y	= _____	_____
2. ex + pense + ive	= _____	_____
3. year + ly	= _____	_____
4. for + ty + es	= _____	_____
5. re + gret + ful	= _____	_____
6. in + quire + y	= _____	_____
7. in + form + ate + ive	= _____	_____
8. un + en + light + en + ed	= _____	_____

Lesson 40 is a test lesson.
There is no worksheet.

Lesson 41

A

1. _____

2. _____

3. _____

B

_____

C

You learned that **cept** and **ceive** are allomorphs. Each word below has a morphograph missing. Use either **ceive** or **cept** to complete each word. Write the entire words. Use your rules.

1. re_____ion

2. incon_____able

3. de_____

4. miscon_____ion

5. de_____ive

6. per_____ed

D

Add the morphographs together.

1. ex + cess + ive   = _____

2. early + est   = _____

3. create + ed   = _____

4. create + ion   = _____

5. fury + ous   = _____

6. con + verse + ate + ion = _____

7. story + es   = _____

8. rain + ing   = _____

E

The English language got its alphabet letters from the Romans. The word for **alphabet** comes from the Greeks. Many words used to describe grammar come from the Romans and Greeks. All of these words came from Greek or Latin: **paragraph, sentence, summary,** and **grammar.**

The word **punctuation** comes from Latin. **Punctu** means point. All the points, or marks you use in writing, are called **punctuation marks.**

All of these words come from Latin: **punctuation mark, question mark, exclamation mark,** and **quotation mark.**

All of these words come from Greek first and then from Latin: **period, comma, asterisk,** and **apostrophe.**

For each punctuation mark, the name of the punctuation mark is given. Write the morphographs that make up the name. You can use Word Parts.

1. " quotation mark = _____ + _____ + _____ mark

2. ? question mark = _____ + _____ mark

3. * asterisk   = _____ + isk

4. ; semicolon   = _____ _____

Answer the items.

5. What letters tell you that **hyphen** came from Greek? _____
   What letters tell you that **apostrophe** came from Greek?

6. What are the morphographs in **punctuate?**   _____

7. What is the first morphograph in **quotation?**   _____

8. The word **exclamation** is related to the word **exclaim.** _____
   What are the morphographs in **exclaim?**

9. The morphograph **semi** means "half" or "almost." A _____
   semicolon is almost a **colon.** What word means
   half circle?

Lesson 42

A

1. _____

2. _____

3. _____

4. _____

B

Make nine real words from the morphographs in the box.

de	scribe	script	ceive	ive	cept	per	ion	pre

1. _____   6. _____

2. _____   7. _____

3. _____   8. _____

4. _____   9. _____

5. _____

C

Write answers for each item.

1. What do you call morphographs that have the same meaning but slightly different spellings?   _____

2. Why is **personnel** spelled with two **n**'s?   _____

3. Is an astrologer a scientist? Is an astronomer a scientist?   _____

4. Write the allomorph of **four.**   _____

5. How do you know that the word **scheme** comes from Greek?   _____

6. How do you know that the word **hyphen** comes from Greek? (There are two clues.)   _____

7. What does the morphograph **in** mean in the word **invisible?**   _____

As you know, a final silent **e** drops when you add a morphograph beginning with a vowel letter. You may have wondered why so many words end with a silent **e.** Here are two reasons:

In many words, the final **e** tells the readers to say the name of a vowel letter in the word. The **e** at the end of **hope** tells us to say the name of the letter **o** when we read that word. The **e** makes sure that you say the word differently from **hop.** The **e** at the end of **pine** makes that word different from **pin.**

Sometimes a final **e** tells us how to say a consonant letter in the word. The letter **c** can be pronounced like a **k** (as in pi**c**ni**c**) or like an **s** (as in pla**c**e). Whenever a **c** is followed by an **e,** you say the **s** sound. Other reasons for a final silent **e** will be given in later lessons.

1. Circle the word in which you would hear the name of a letter.

   gath   gathe

2. These words confuse many people. Circle the two words in which you hear the name of a letter.

   breath   breathe   clothe   cloth

3. Circle the words from this list that have a letter **c** with the sound of **s.**

   trace   vice   pick   race   juice   police

   track   arc   voice   panic   nice   ace

Lesson 43

A

1. _____   11. _____
2. _____   12. _____
3. _____   13. _____
4. _____   14. _____
5. _____   15. _____
6. _____   16. _____
7. _____   17. _____
8. _____   18. _____
9. _____   19. _____
10. _____   20. _____

B

Find the misspelled words in the student's answer. Then write those words correctly.

The city of Perth is the capital of Western Australia. The most important feature of Perth's geography is the beautiful Swan River. Many parks and gardens are located throughout the city and along the river. The weather is usually sunny and warm. People who live in Perth enjoy the opportunity to take part in outdoor sports and hobbies such as tennis and photography. Visitors to the city do not feel like strangers for long because the people who live there are so friendly.

Why is Perth an ideal city for people who love the outdoors? _____

Perth has good whether so peeple who love the outdoors can spend a lot of time in the sun. They can viset gardens and parks or walk along the Swan River. People who like photografy can take many pictures of the river and other things. All these oppertunities make Perth an ideel city for people who like to do things outdoors.

_____

_____

_____

_____

_____

C

Write the correct spelling for each word. Then write one of these letters after each word:

Write **O** if the word is spelled by just putting the morphographs together.
Write **A** if the final-**e** rule explains why the spelling is changed.
Write **B** if the doubling rule explains why the spelling is changed.
Write **C** if the **y**-to-**i** rule explains why the spelling is changed.

		word	rule
1.	re + fuse + al	= _____	_____
2.	in + fury + ate	= _____	_____
3.	create + ure	= _____	_____
4.	re + fer + ing	= _____	_____
5.	in + volve + ment	= _____	_____
6.	myst + er + y + ous + ly	= _____	_____
7.	simple + y	= _____	_____
8.	re + marry + ed	= _____	_____

D

Write the morphographs for each word.

1. _____ + _____ + _____ = dictation
2. _____ + _____ + _____ + _____ = observation
3. _____ + _____ + _____ + _____ = conversation
4. _____ + _____ + _____ + _____ = presentation
5. _____ + s = clothes
6. _____ + _____ + _____ = enclosure

Lesson 44

A

proceed   procedure   precede   precedent   antecedent

B

1. _____

2. _____

3. _____

4. _____

C

Some of the most frequently misspelled words have the allomorphs **cede** or **ceed.** Although the allomorphs are spelled two different ways, they have the same meanings: "to move" or "to yield."

If you remember some facts about **cede** and **ceed,** you will never misspell words like con**cede,** pro**ceed,** or inter**cede.**

The allomorph spelled **ceed** takes only three prefixes. These are **pro, ex,** and **suc.** For all other prefixes use the allomorph spelled **cede.** (There is only one exception to these facts. The word **procedure** is spelled with only one **e,** but other words that begin with **proceed** are spelled with two **e**'s, like **proceeding** and **proceeded.**)

Choose **cede** or **ceed,** and then add the morphographs together.

1. suc + cede/ceed   = _____

2. re + cede/ceed   = _____

3. ex + cede/ceed + ed   = _____

4. pro + cede/ceed   = _____

5. pre + cede/ceed + ence = _____

6. ante + cede/ceed + ent = _____

Four words are misspelled. Write those words correctly.

7. succeding	12. recede	_____
8. exceeds	13. precedent	
9. interceeded	14. conceed	_____
10. proceeded	15. antecedent	
11. procedure	16. preceed	_____

_____

A student wrote this story. Seven words are misspelled. Write each of those words correctly.

My freind created a monster. The creture was six feat tall and wieghed a lot. The creature ate all the houses on our street. My friend was very woried, and her parents were furyous. The monster was very espensive to make, but my friend had to give it away.

_____

_____

_____

_____   _____

_____   _____

E

The morphograph **pre** means "before." The morphograph **pre** is a prefix because it come before other morphographs. Four words in this exercise have the prefix **pre.** Add the morphographs together.

1. pre + dict + able = _____

2. breath + less + ness = _____

3. ad + mit + ing = _____

4. heal + th + y + er = _____

5. pre + sent + ate + ion = _____

6. pre + view + ing = _____

7. in + dis + pense + able = _____

8. pre + pare + ed = _____

Lesson 45 is a test lesson.
There is no worksheet.

Lesson 46

A

1. _____

2. _____

3. _____

B

The Greeks have a letter for **r** called **rho.** The Greeks make a mark by the letter **rho** in some words to tell the speaker to pronounce the **r** with an **h** sound. When Romans borrowed words from Greek, they spelled these words with the letters **rh.**

We still have their strange spelling in some words: **rh**ythm, **rh**ubarb, **rh**apsody.

The morphograph **rhino** means "nose." The morphograph **ceros** means "horn." A rhinoceros is an animal with a horn on its nose.

The word **rhyme** used to be spelled **rime.** But people thought **rime** must be a misspelling. They thought **rime** should be spelled like **rhythm,** so they changed the spelling to **rhyme.**

Add the morphographs together.

1. rhythm + ic   = _____

2. rhetor + ic   = _____

3. rheum + ate + ism = _____

4. rhino + ceros   = _____

5. rhyme + ing   = _____

Answer the items.

6. What are the different spellings for the **r** sounds   _____
   in **rhinoceros?**

7. What are the different spellings for the **r** sounds   _____
   in **rhubarb?**

8. **Rhino** is a shorter word for which animal?   _____

9. The morphograph **rrhea** means to flow.
Rhinorrhea is a medical term for a very
runny ____.

_____

10. The word **rhythm** comes from Greek.
How do you know? (There are 2 clues.)

_____

11. The word **rhyme** does not come from Greek.
Why is it spelled with **rh?**

_____

C

Write the morphographs for each word.

1. _____ + _____ = furious

2. _____ + _____ + _____ = transmitting

3. _____ + _____ = transit

4. _____ + _____ = summit

D

You have learned a rule about using the allomorphs **cede** and **ceed**. **Ceed** follows the prefixes
pro, ex, and **suc.** All other prefixes take **cede**. The only exception is the word **procedure.**

Choose **ceed** or **cede,** and then add the morphographs together.

1. ante + cede/ceed + ent   = _____

2. suc + cede/ceed + ed   = _____

3. ex + cede/ceed + ing + ly = _____

4. re + cede/ceed + ing   = _____

5. pre + cede/ceed + ed   = _____

6. pro + cede/ceed + ing + s = _____

7. con + cede/ceed + s   = _____

8. pro + cede/ceed + ure   = _____

Lesson 47

Add the morphographs together.

1. pre + cede + ent   = _____

2. pre + script + ion   = _____

3. re + serve + ate + ion = _____

4. rhyme + ed   = _____

5. re + sent + ment   = _____

6. pro + cede + ure   = _____

7. scheme + ing   = _____

8. pre + fer +ed   = _____

The English word **sentence** means "a group of words that begin with a capital letter and end with an ending mark." The Romans had a different meaning for this word. **Sentence** comes from the morphograph **sent** that means "to feel." This was the meaning used in Latin. In Latin, a sentence was an opinion or a feeling that somebody had. A sentence could be a story, a paragraph, or one line.

We still use the word **sentence** to mean "an opinion." If a court of law judges a person to be guilty of a crime, the person is **sentenced.** The **sentence** the person receives may be five years in prison, or it may be a month in jail.

Answer the items.

1. Write the morphographs in **sentence.**   _____

2. What does the first morphograph in **sentence** mean?   _____

3. What did the word **sentence** mean in Latin?   _____

4. This item has an English meaning of **sentence:** She wrote a lovely **sentence.** What meaning of **sentence** is that?   _____

5. This item has an English meaning of **sentence:** The judge will give her **sentence** tomorrow. What meaning of **sentence** is that?   _____

C

Write the answers for each item.

1. What are the different spellings for the **r** sounds in **rhinoceros?** _____

2. Write the allomorph for **cept.** _____

3. Write the two words in which you hear the name of a letter. _____

   breath   breathe
   clothe   cloth

4. The word **rhythm** comes from Greek. How do you know? (There are 2 clues.) _____

5. Which three prefixes take the allomorph **ceed?** _____

D

Circle the misspelled word in each group. Then write it correctly.

1.	2.	3.	4.
duration	repellent	committment	dictionary
aproach	rephrased	summary	breathless
visible	imagenary	succeeded	compelled
military	wonderful	rebellion	exercize
_____	_____	_____	_____

Lesson 48

1. _____

2. _____

B

Make twelve real words from the morphographs in the box.

| con | pre | ed | ceed | ex | cede | suc | pro | ing |

1. _____   7. _____

2. _____   8. _____

3. _____   9. _____

4. _____   10. _____

5. _____   11. _____

6. _____   12. _____

C

Write the morphographs for each word.

1. _____ + _____ = divide

2. _____ + _____ + _____ + _____ = individual

3. _____ + _____ = weighed

4. _____ + t = weight

5. _____ + _____ + _____ = meaningless

6. _____ + _____ = meant

D

The words listed below come from Greek. In each word there are two clues that tell you the word is of Greek origin. Underline the clues in each word.

For example, the word **physical** has **ph** and a **y** between two consonants. When you write **physical,** underline these clues: **ph y**sical.

Remember that **ph, rh, ch,** and **y** between two consonants can all be clues.

1. rhythm

2. phonograph

3. psychology

4. morphograph

5. hyphen

6. synonym

7. physicist

8. symphony

E

Find the misspelled words in these sentences. Then write the words correctly.

1. Her describtion was very graphic. _____

2. Some spies work on hazerdous buziness. _____

3. The originel information was lost durring the disaster. _____

4. The author planed to revize the mannuscript. _____

5. We're hopping that she will succede. _____

Lesson 49

Circle the misspelled word in each group. Then write it correctly.

1. admit
   really
   controled
   misspelling
   _____

2. spelled
   studying
   allotted
   decieved
   _____

3. synonim
   proceeded
   enjoyable
   noisier
   _____

4. thoughtful
   buried
   perscription
   perceptive
   _____

5. telegraph
   exceedingly
   loneliness
   akquired
   _____

6. casual
   replied
   symbowl
   scheme
   _____

B

Write the correct spelling for each word. Then write one of these letters after each word:

Write **O** if the word is spelled by just putting the morphographs together.
Write **A** if the final-**e** rule explains why the spelling is changed.
Write **B** if the doubling rule explains why the spelling is changed.
Write **C** if the **y**-to-**i** rule explains why the spelling is changed.

	word	**rule**
1. op + pose + ite	= _____	_____
2. rhythm + ic + al	= _____	_____
3. sym + phone + y	= _____	_____
4. ex + er + cise + s	= _____	_____
5. o + miss + ion + s	= _____	_____
6. family + ar + ize	= _____	_____
7. re + mit + ance	= _____	_____
8. dict + ion + ary + es	= _____	_____
9. heal + th + y + er	= _____	_____
10. sur + face + ed	= _____	_____

C

Write the word for each meaning clue.

weak   prefix   pear   citation   fourth   summit

1. a ticket   _____

2. 4th   _____

3. a certain fruit   _____

4. the highest part of a mountain   _____

5. a morphograph that comes before other morphographs   _____

6. not strong   _____

Lesson 50 is a test lesson.
There is no worksheet.

Lesson 51

A

Here is the final-vowel rule: Drop the final vowel from a morphograph when the next morphograph begins with a vowel.

1. manu + age   = _____
2. sacri + ed   = _____
3. sacri + fice = _____
4. equi + al   = _____
5. symbol + ic   = _____
6. punctu + ure = _____
7. mode + est   = _____
8. manu + script = _____

B

The coarse clouds will affect the weather.

C

Write the morphographs for each word.

1. _____ + _____ + _____ + _____ = individual
2. _____ + _____ + _____ + _____ = disciplinary
3. _____ + _____ + _____ = sentenced
4. _____ + _____ = business
5. e + _____ = event
6. _____ + _____ + _____ = eventual

D

The morphograph **fine (fin)** may refer to completing something or putting it inside boundaries. Here are some words that use the morphograph **fine (fin)**.

final: The final thing you do is the ending thing you do, or the last thing you do.

finish: When you finish something, you complete it.

confined: When something is confined, it is put inside boundaries.

define: When you define something, you use words to make meaning boundaries.

Write the morphographs for each word.

1. _____ + _____ + _____ = confined

2. _____ + _____ = finish

3. _____ + _____ + _____ = finally

4. _____ + _____ + _____ + _____ = undefined

Write the correct words containing the morphograph **fine (fin).**

5. I'm almost done with this book. Right now I'm on the _____ chapter.

6. I will probably _____ it within an hour.

7. During the day the dog was _____ to his crate.

8. He tried to _____ seven words.

9. She will try to _____ her report on time.

E

Write the correct word or words for each sentence.

1. He bought a **peace/piece** of cloth. _____

2. We'll **meat/meet hear/here** at noon. _____

Lesson 52

A

Here is the final-vowel rule: Drop the final vowel from a morphograph when the next morphograph begins with a vowel.

1. sta + ate = _____
2. manu + age = _____
3. manu + script = _____
4. press + ure = _____

5. contra + dict = _____
6. equi + nox = _____
7. contra + ary = _____
8. equi + ate = _____

B

The coarse clouds will affect the weather.

C

Find the misspelled words in these sentences. Then write the words correctly.

1. The author wrote four imaginetive storys. _____
2. Chris suceeded in deceiving everyone. _____
3. The dizaster occured fourty minutes ago. _____
4. His question embarassed us. _____

D

In Lesson 51 you learned that the morphograph **fine (fin)** refers to completing something or putting it inside boundaries. Here are some more words with the morphograph **fine (fin)**.

finite: Something that is finite is within the boundaries of things we can count.

definite: If something is definite, its boundaries are very clear. It is not vague.

infinite: Things that are infinite are beyond the boundaries of things we can count. The number of stars is infinite, meaning we cannot count them all.

definition: You make a definition when you describe or explain something exactly.

People often misspell words like **definitely** because they don't know that the word is related to other words with the morphograph **fine (fin).** If you know that the word is made of **fine (fin) + ite,** you know it has to be spelled **definitely,** even though you don't hear the sounds the way you do in the word **finite.**

Write the morphographs for each word.

1. _____ + _____ = finite

2. _____ + _____ + _____ = definite

3. _____ + _____ + _____ = infinite

4. _____ + _____ + _____ + _____ = definition

5. _____ + _____ + _____ + _____ + _____ = indefinitely

Write the correct words containing **fine (fin).**

6. They want to go to Hawaii, but their plans are not yet _____.

7. There seems to be an _____ number of stars. I can never count them all.

8. Whenever I invite him to a party, he always says "Maybe" or "Perhaps." He never gives me a _____ answer.

9. The opposite of **infinite** is _____.

10. If you don't know what a word means, a dictionary is a good place to look for its _____.

Lesson 53

A

Here is the final-vowel rule: Drop the final vowel from a morphograph when the next morphograph begins with a vowel.

1. ob + via + ous = _____
2. sta + ate + ment = _____
3. manu + fact + ure = _____
4. con + sta + ant = _____
5. se + pare + ate = _____
6. sacri + lege + ious = _____
7. de + via + ate = _____
8. mis + manu + age = _____
9. ad + equi + ate = _____
10. contra + dict = _____

B

_____

C

1. _____ 5. _____
2. _____ 6. _____
3. _____ 7. _____
4. _____ 8. _____

D

Make eight real words from the morphographs in the box.

| al | de | ite | fine | in | ly | ish |

1. _____   5. _____

2. _____   6. _____

3. _____   7. _____

4. _____   8. _____

E

The letters **tw** are often used as a short form of the word **two.** Here are some words with **tw: tw**enty, **tw**ice, **tw**ilight, **tw**elve, **tw**in, and be**tw**een. You don't hear the sound "tw" in the word **two,** but you hear it in these other words.

Write the missing word for each sentence.

1. There are _____ months in a year.

2. The fighting _____ the two countries continued for years.

3. Two people who are born at the same time are called _____.

4. She tried it once, but he tried it _____.

5. She had trouble seeing things in the _____.

6. When you do something twice, you do it _____ times.

7. Ten plus two is _____. Ten times two is _____.

F

Write the morphographs for each word.

1. _____ + _____ = surface

2. _____ + _____ = profess

3. _____ + mode + _____ = commodity

4. _____ + _____ + _____ = rephrased

5. _____ + _____ + _____ = opportune

6. _____ + _____ = compare

Lesson 54

A

1. _____

2. _____

B

1. equi + vale + ent   = _____

2. sta + ate + ion   = _____

3. contra + dict + ion = _____

4. pre + via + ous   = _____

5. di + sta + ance   = _____

6. en + dure + ance   = _____

7. sacri + fice + ial = _____

8. manu + fact + ure   = _____

C

A student wrote this report. Ten words are misspelled. Write each of those words correctly.

Exercise is very important if you want to be healthy and phisically fit. Running and swimming are to good forms of exersise. For both sports, you have to learn to breath right. Excessive running, when you are not used to it, can hurt you. You must disipline yourself to run short distinces. Find a good book that discribes how to start runing. Make inquiryes among your friends who run. Then start running. You may get an occasional ache or pain, but if you do it right, the occurences of your pains will become fewer and fewer.

_____

_____

_____

_____

_____

_____

_____

_____

D

Manu and mani are allomorphs. The morphograph manu means "hand" in these words: manuscript, manual. The words manicure, manipulate, and manifest contain the morphograph mani.

Write the morphographs for each word.

1. _____ + _____ = manual

2. _____ + pule + _____ = manipulate

3. _____ + _____ + ate + _____ = manifestation

4. _____ + _____ = manuscript

5. _____ + _____ = manicure

6. _____ + _____ + _____ = manufacture

Answer the items.

7. Look at these words: **sacrifice/sacrament.** _____
   Write the allomorph for **sacri.**

8. Write the allomorph for **manu.** _____

9. The morphograph **pedi** means feet. _____
   When you have your fingernails shaped,
   you have a **manicure.** What word means
   having your toenails shaped?

E

Write the word for each meaning clue.

affect	twenty-two	coarse	definite	infinite	twice

1. two times _____

2. rough and ragged _____

3. beyond the boundaries of things we can count _____

4. not vague _____

5. make it change _____

6. 22 _____

Lesson 55 is a test lesson.
There is no worksheet.

Lesson 56

A

1. _____

2. _____

B

1. sta + ate + ment   = _____

2. via + duct   = _____

3. fine + al   = _____

4. equi + ate + ion   = _____

5. con + cluse + ive   = _____

6. pre + via + ous   = _____

7. sta + able   = _____

8. e + sta + able + ish = _____

C

Most of the people in Australia, Canada, Great Britain, and the United States speak the same language—English. Although many English words are pronounced differently in these countries, most of the words are spelled the same. There are, however, some differences.

One man in the United States was almost entirely responsible for those differences. His name was Noah Webster. Webster started writing dictionaries about 200 years ago. He thought many English words were not spelled the way they sounded, so he changed the spellings. For example, Webster spelled the words **build** and **laugh** like this: **bild, laf.**

Most people did not like these new spellings, so they didn't use them. Some of Webster's spellings, however, became widely used in the United States and in parts of Canada. The lists show some of those words.

How the words are spelled in Australia, Great Britain, and parts of Canada:		How the words are spelled in the United States and parts of Canada:	
grey	tyre	gray	tire
mould	programme	mold	program
colour	plough	color	plow
favourite	humour	favorite	humor
centre	glamour	center	glamor

Use the words from the lists to complete the sentences below. Use the spelling that is most common where you live. If you are not sure which spelling to use, look up the word in the dictionary, or ask your teacher.

1. My grandfather's hair turned _____ when he was very young.

2. The only _____ my sister likes is blue.

3. In some parts of the world, farmers still use horses or oxen to _____ their fields.

4. Marie can cheer up anyone with her terrific sense of _____.

5. My bicycle has a flat _____.

6. Dessert is my _____ part of a meal.

7. The name of this spelling _____ is Spelling Mastery.

8. Bob put flowers in the _____ of the table.

D

Write the morphographs for each word.

1. _____ + _____ + ious = sacrilegious

2. _____ + _____ = sacrament

3. _____ + _____ + _____ + _____ = conversation

4. _____ + _____ = manicure

5. _____ + _____ + _____ = reversal

6. _____ + _____ + _____ + _____ = manifestation

Lesson 57

1. patri + on = _____
2. sacri + fice = _____
3. manu + age = _____
4. tele + phone = _____
5. a + muse + ment = _____
6. equi + al + ly = _____
7. ob + via + ous + ly = _____
8. equi + di + sta + ant = _____

B

The principal gave me advice.

C

Write the correct spelling for each word. Then write one of these letters after each word:

Write **O** if the word is spelled by just putting the morphographs together.
Write **A** if the final-vowel rule explains why the spelling is changed.
Write **B** if the doubling rule explains why the spelling is changed.
Write **C** if the **y**-to-**i** rule explains why the spelling is changed.

	word	rule
1. manu + age =	_____	_____
2. verse + ion =	_____	_____
3. manu + script =	_____	_____
4. vary + able =	_____	_____
5. in + sta + ant =	_____	_____
6. en + dure + ance =	_____	_____
7. sacra + ment =	_____	_____
8. study + ed =	_____	_____

Find the misspelled words in the student's answer. Then write those words correctly.

Dolphins are excellent swimmers. They are also extraordinary leapers. One scientist wondered why they occasionally travel over the water in huge, ten-foot leaps, when they can swim through it with so little effort. Are they just having fun?

The scientist measured the size and weight of the dolphins, the speed at which they swim, and the distance they leap. He made an amazing discovery. By leaping out of the water, the dolphins were saving energy. The faster a dolphin tries to swim, the more work it has to do to get through the water. Once it reaches a certain speed, the dolphin can actually save energy by hurling itself into the air, which does not drag against the dolphin the way water does.

Why do dolphins leap?

By taking measurements of speed, wait, and distence, a sientist found out how hard a dolphin works when it's swimming. His calclations showed that above a certian speed, it is easyer to jump into the air than travel thorough water. Leaping saves energy.

_____

_____

_____

_____

_____

_____

_____

Lesson 58

A

Write the correct spelling for each word. Then write one of these letters after each word:

Write **O** if the word is spelled by just putting the morphographs together.
Write **A** if the final-vowel rule explains why the spelling is changed.
Write **B** if the doubling rule explains why the spelling is changed.
Write **C** if the **y**-to-**i** rule explains why the spelling is changed.

		word	rule
1.	swim + er	= _____	_____
2.	radio + ate	= _____	_____
3.	patri + on + ize	= _____	_____
4.	pro + pel + er	= _____	_____
5.	equi + ate + or	= _____	_____
6.	radio + loge + y	= _____	_____
7.	in + fury + ate	= _____	_____
8.	chang + ing	= _____	_____

B

The principal gave me advice.

C

Here is the final-vowel rule: Drop the final vowel from a morphograph when the next morphograph begins with a vowel, unless you hear both vowel sounds.

1.	punctu + ate	= _____
2.	patri + on	= _____
3.	patri + ot	= _____
4.	sta + ble	= _____
5.	radio + ant	= _____
6.	manu + al	= _____
7.	radio + act + ive	= _____
8.	patri + arch	= _____

D

The morphograph **migra** means "to wander." Here are some words that use the morphograph **migra.**

migrate: Migrate means to move to a new location.

migrant: Something that is wandering is migrant. A person who wanders is a migrant.

emigrate: The morphograph **e** means "away or out." When you leave your country, you emigrate.

immigrate: The morphograph **im** means "in or into." When you immigrate, you come to a new home in a new country.

migratory: Animals that migrate are migratory animals.

Write the morphographs for each word.

1. _____ + _____ = migrate

2. _____ + _____ = migrant

3. _____ + _____ + _____ = immigrant

4. _____ + _____ + _____ = emigrant

5. _____ + _____ + _____ + _____ = immigration

6. _____ + _____ + ory = migratory

Write the answer for each item.

7. Why does **immigrate** have two **m**'s? _____

8. What does the morphograph **im** mean? _____

9. What does the morphograph **e** mean? _____

Write the correct words using **migra.**

10. The pilgrims _____ from Europe because they were not happy there.

11. Some birds _____ thousands of miles every year.

12. In 1788 the first European _____ came to Australia.

Lesson 59

A

B

Here is the final-vowel rule: Drop the final vowel from a morphograph when the next morphograph begins with a vowel, unless you hear both vowel sounds.

1. vacu + ate   = _____

2. e + vacu + ate   = _____

3. muse + um   = _____

4. im + migra + ant = _____

5. punctu +ure   = _____

6. contra + ary   = _____

7. punctu + al   = _____

8. muse + ic   = _____

C

1. _____

2. _____

D

You know that some words are spelled two different ways in different countries. For example, people in Australia and Great Britain use the spelling **colour.** People in the United States use the spelling **color.** Both spellings are used in Canada.

Circle the spelling that is more appropriate for where you live. If you are not sure which spelling to use, look up the word in a dictionary, or ask your teacher.

1. armor/armour

2. harbour/harbor

3. favour/favor

4. labor/labour

5. flavour/flavor

6. color/colour

7. vapor/vapour

8. honor/honour

9. neighbor/neighbour

10. behaviour/behavior

11. valour/valor

12. odor/odour

13. humor/humour

14. glamour/glamor

Circle the misspelled word in each group. Then write it correctly.

1. patronage
   dictionary
   manicure
   imigrate

   _____

2. sacrifice
   infuriate
   misstake
   conscientious

   _____

3. permitted
   conceive
   radial
   instint

   _____

4. equator
   embarrass
   defenition
   sacrament

   _____

5. station
   referral
   twinty
   finally

   _____

6. glorious
   pleasure
   obviously
   equil

   _____

7. establish
   afect
   sacrilege
   confined

   _____

8. denial
   unfortunat
   health
   distance

   _____

Lesson 60 is a test lesson.
There is no worksheet.

Lesson 61

A

1. _____

2. _____

B

Add the morphographs together.

1. re + act + ion   = _____

2. sta + ate + ion   = _____

3. coarse + ly   = _____

4. de + part + ment + al = _____

5. manu + age + er + ial = _____

6. radio + ate + ion   = _____

7. manu + fact + ure   = _____

8. equi + vale + ence   = _____

9. a + muse + ment   = _____

10. ob + via + ous + ly = _____

C

Write the correct spelling for each word. Then write one of these letters after each word:

Write **O** if the word is spelled by just putting the morphographs together.
Write **A** if the final-vowel rule explains why the spelling is changed.
Write **B** if the doubling rule explains why the spelling is changed.
Write **C** if the **y**-to-**i** rule explains why the spelling is changed.

	word	**rule**
1. trans + fer + ed =		
2. clear + ance =		
3. muse + um =		
4. muse + ic + ian =		
5. di + sta + ance =		
6. weigh + t =		
7. carry + ing =		
8. vacu + ant =		

D

Write the correct word or words for each sentence.

1. They have been married for **to/two** years. _____

2. Kim can fly a **plain/plane.** _____

3. Jesse gathered **wood/would** for the fire. _____

4. The **meat/meet** was on **sail/sale.** _____

Lesson 62

A

1. _____
2. _____
3. _____
4. _____
5. _____
6. _____
7. _____
8. _____
9. _____
10. _____
11. _____
12. _____
13. _____

14. _____
15. _____
16. _____
17. _____
18. _____
19. _____
20. _____
21. _____
22. _____
23. _____
24. _____
25. _____

B

Write morphographs for each word. Put a + between the morphographs.

1. reporter _____
2. clearance _____
3. recommended _____
4. evacuate _____
5. amusement _____
6. sacrilege _____
7. exceedingly _____
8. excessively _____

Circle the misspelled words in these sentences. Then write the words correctly.

1. The creature was raydioactive. _____

2. The preformance was amuzing. _____

3. We approached the barial cite at twilight. _____

The morphograph **ify** means "to make." Here are some words with the morphograph **ify.**

simplify: When you make something simpler, you simplify it.

classify: When you put things into groups or classes, you classify them.

falsify: When you make something false or lie about it, you falsify that thing.

justify: When you give reasons why your actions are right, you justify your actions.

Write the morphographs for each word.

1. _____ + _____ = falsify

2. _____ + _____ + _____ = classified

3. _____ + _____ + _____ = simplifying

4. _____ + _____ + _____ + _____ = unjustifiable

Write the correct words with the morphograph **ify.**

5. This explanation is too hard for me to understand. Can you _____ it for me?

6. He always tries to _____ his actions so they seem reasonable.

7. Some people _____ food into four groups: meat, dairy products, fruits-vegetables, and cereals.

8. People who _____ their records could face jail time.

For each word below make up a word that ends in **ify.** Example: **notice—notify.**

9. identity _____

10. signal _____

11. intensive _____

12. mode _____

13. horrible _____

Lesson 63

A

Stationery is on sale in aisle two.

B

Add the morphographs together. Remember to use your spelling rules.

1. sta + ate + ment = _____
2. ex + pedi + ent = _____
3. origin + al = _____
4. equi + ate + ion = _____
5. pedi + al = _____
6. re + e + sta + able + ish = _____
7. simple + ice + ity = _____
8. simple + ify + ed = _____

C

For each word below make up a word that ends in **ify.** Example: **glorious—glorify.**

1. quality _____   3. identical _____
2. terrible _____   4. mystical _____

D

You have learned the word **malediction** and what it means. A **malediction** is "speaking badly about, or a curse." The part of **malediction** that you know is **dict.** That part means "speech or speak." The part that you don't know is **male.** You know that **malediction** is "something that is very bad or evil." So you may be able to figure out that **male (mal)** means "evil or harmful." Below are some words that use the morphograph **male.**

malice: We say that an evil person is full of malice. An evil person is malicious.

malady: Malady is another word for sickness or a harmful disease.

malignant: When something is malignant, it is very harmful or dangerous.

Write morphographs for each word.

1. _____ + _____ = malice

2. _____ + _____ + ious = malicious

3. _____ + ade + _____ = malady

4. _____ + ign + _____ = malignant

Write the correct words with **male.**

5. We were so relieved when the doctor told us Mother did not have a _____ growth.

6. She is very sick now, but she hasn't had that _____ for very long.

7. He did so many evil things that we knew he was a _____ person.

8. Although her life has been very rough, she is not full of _____.

E

A student wrote this report. Nine words are misspelled. Write each of those words correctly.

When we went to the museum Sunday, we discoverred that it was closed. There was a notice on the door from the management. The notise said that the managment regretted imforming its partrins that the muzeum wood be closed indefinately. Before it could be reopened, certain repairs had to be made on the building.

We were very disapointed.

_____

_____

_____

_____

_____

_____   _____   _____

Lesson 64

A

<u>benign</u>   <u>beneficial</u>   benevolent   malice   malicious

B

Stationery is on sale in aisle two.

C

1. _____

2. _____

D

Write the morphographs for each word. Put a + between the morphographs.

1. original _____

2. submit _____

3. museum _____

4. vacuum _____

5. malice _____

6. malicious _____

7. station _____

8. nutrient _____

You have learned that **male** means "bad or evil." The opposite of **male** is **bene.** You already know that a benediction is speaking well of or a blessing. Below are some words that use the morphograph **bene.**

benevolent: A benevolent person is a good or kind person.

benefit: Something that benefits you is good for you.

benefactor: A benefactor is a person who is good to other people or who benefits them.

benign: If something is benign, it is not harmful. If a diseased part is benign, it is not malignant. It will not harm you.

beneficial: Something that is beneficial for you is good for you.

Write the morphographs for each word.

1. _____ + _____ = benefit

2. _____ + vole + _____ = benevolent

3. _____ + _____ = benign

4. _____ + _____ + _____ = benefactor

5. _____ + fice + _____ = beneficial

6. _____ + _____ + _____ = benediction

Write the correct words with **bene.**

7. The growth on Mother's leg is not malignant. It is _____.

8. A lot of sleep is _____ for babies.

9. My aunt is so helpful and kind. She is the most _____ person I know.

10. Sandra hopes that her experiences abroad will really _____ her.

11. His father is very kind to many people. Those people call him a _____.

Lesson 65 is a test lesson.
There is no worksheet.

Lesson 66

A

_____

_____

B

1. _____

2. _____

C

Add the morphographs together.

1. peri + il   = _____

2. nutri + ite + ion   = _____

3. e + duce + ate   = _____

4. spy + ed   = _____

5. e + spy + on + age = _____

6. ex + pedi + ite   = _____

7. ex + peri + ment   = _____

8. de + via + ate + ion = _____

D

Write the correct spelling for each word. Then write one of these letters after each word:

Write **O** if the word is spelled by just putting the morphographs together.
Write **A** if the final-vowel rule explains why the spelling is changed.
Write **B** if the doubling rule explains why the spelling is changed.
Write **C** if the **y**-to-**i** rule explains why the spelling is changed.

		word	rule
1. bene + ign	=	_____	_____
2. im + pedi + ment	=	_____	_____
3. pedi + al	=	_____	_____
4. af + fect + ion	=	_____	_____

	word	rule
5. bene + fice + ial =	_____	_____
6. of + fice + ial =	_____	_____
7. class + ify + ing =	_____	_____
8. non + com + mit + al =	_____	_____

E

A frequently misspelled word is **sandwich.** The spelling of the word is easier if you know the word's origin. The word **sandwich** came from someone's name, so **sandwich** is a single-morphograph word. The man was an Englishman named John Montague. He was the **Earl of Sandwich.** The earl loved to play cards and play pool. He was so involved with his games that he would sometimes go for more than a day without stopping to sleep. He was too impatient to sit down for a meal, so he invented the sandwich. He did this by putting a piece of meat between two slices of bread. He did not need a knife and fork to eat it.

Answer the items.

1. Who invented the **sandwich?** _____

2. Some people spell **sandwich** this way: **sandwitch.** They do this because they think **sandwich** has two morphographs. Which two morphographs do they think it has?

   _____

3. How many morphographs are in the word **sandwich?**

   _____

4. The word **sandal** is a single-morphograph word. It came from the Greek word for a wooden shoe—**sandalion.** Many people think **sandal** is made of two morphographs. If it were, what two morphographs would you use to make **sandal?**

   _____

Lesson 67

conscious   conscience   scientist   conscientious

1. _____

2. _____

spacious   nutritious   malicious   cautious   vicious

Write the correct spelling for each word. Then write one of these letters after each word:

Write **O** if the word is spelled by just putting the morphographs together.
Write **A** if the final-vowel rule explains why the spelling is changed.
Write **B** if the doubling rule explains why the spelling is changed.
Write **C** if the **y**-to-**i** rule explains why the spelling is changed.

		word	rule
1.	ident + ify + ed	= _____	_____
2.	sandwich + es	= _____	_____
3.	bene + fice + ial	= _____	_____
4.	of + fice	= _____	_____
5.	auto + bio + graph + ic + al	= _____	_____
6.	pedi + al	= _____	_____
7.	re + gret + able	= _____	_____
8.	of + fice + ial	= _____	_____

Circle the misspelled word in each group. Then write it correctly.

1. manifested	2. obvious	3. deviate	4. experiment
beneficial	impedament	education	stationery
clasified	direction	benevolent	equaly
spies	vacuum	maliss	twenty-four

_____ _____ _____ _____

You may have learned that **science** is a single morphograph word. Actually, it is made up of two morphographs—**sci** plus **ence.** This passage tells more about the morphograph **sci.**

The morphograph **sci** means "to know." This morphograph is pronounced different ways, but it is always spelled the same way. And its spelling does not follow the final-vowel rule.

The morphograph **sci** is pronounced "sigh" in some words. In other words, it makes the sound "sh." In the words below, **sci** sounds like "sigh."

science: The organization of knowledge is called science.

scientist: Someone who has special knowledge or is looking for knowledge is called a scientist.

scientific: Something that is related to science is scientific.

In the words below, **sci** sounds like "sh."

conscious: If your mind is awake and you know what's going on around you, you are conscious.

conscience: Your conscience is the part of your mind that knows right from wrong.

conscientious: If you work hard, you are conscientious.

Regardless of the way **sci** is pronounced, the **i** in **sci** never drops. When we add **sci** to **ence,** the vowel does not drop. Sci + ence is spelled **science.** Remember, **sci** may be pronounced two ways, but the **i** never drops. If you remember that rule, you will be able to spell four of the most commonly misspelled words. They are **science, conscious, conscientious,** and **conscience.**

Write the morphographs for each word.

1. _____ + _____ + _____ = conscience

2. _____ + _____ + _____ + _____ = unconscious

3. _____ + _____ = science

4. _____ + _____ + _____ + _____ = conscientious

5. _____ + _____ + ist = scientist

Write the correct words containing **sci.**

6. Her _____ wouldn't let her steal the pie.

7. Biology and chemistry are branches of _____.

8. A hard blow on his head knocked him _____.

Lesson 68

A

conscient<u>ious</u>   grac<u>ious</u>   consc<u>ious</u>   cautious   vicious

B

_____   _____   _____

C

Make eight real words from the morphographs in the box.

migra   ate   radio   ant   vacu   ion   equi

1. _____   5. _____
2. _____   6. _____
3. _____   7. _____
4. _____   8. _____

D

In words that come from Latin, the letters **q-u** act like two consonants, not like a consonant and a vowel. Words that come from Latin are easy to identify. The letters **q-u** make the sound "kw" in these words. Because the letters **q-u** stand for two consonant sounds, we treat **q-u** as two consonants. Remember that if the letters make the sound "kw," they are two consonants.

The **q-u** in the word **quit** makes the "kw" sound. So the word **quit** is a consonant, consonant, vowel, consonant. The word is a short word that ends **cvc**. Because **quit** ends **cvc**, the final consonant doubles in words like **quitter, quitting,** and **acquittal.** Remember that if the letters **q-u** are pronounced "kw," they are two consonants.

The underlined parts of the morphographs below end **cvc**:

q<u>uiz</u> + ed = quizzed   e + q<u>uip</u> + ed = equipped

Like most short morphographs that end **cvc,** the final **c** is doubled when the next morphograph begins with a **v.**

1. Why does the **t** double in the word **quitter?** _____

2. Why doesn't the **r** double in the word **inquired?** _____

3. Why doesn't the **t** double in the word **quieter?** _____

4. Why does the **z** double in the word **quizzed?** _____

Combine the morphographs.

5. e + quip + ment = _____

6. quiz + ic + al = _____

7. quote + ed = _____

8. ac + quit + ed = _____

9. ac + quire + ed = _____

10. quit + ing = _____

E

Write the answers for each item.

1. A **benevolent** person is a good or kind person. _____
   What is a **malevolent** person?

2. What does the morphograph **bene** mean? _____

3. Does the **i** ever drop from the morphograph **sci?** _____

4. Who invented the **sandwich?** _____

Lesson 69

A

verse   virtue   tract   fort

B

_____   _____   _____

C

stren<u>uous</u>   virt<u>uous</u>   vac<u>uous</u>   continuous   conspicuous

D

_____

E

Add the morphographs together.

1. space + ious   = _____

2. grace + ious + ness   = _____

3. dis + ap + pear + ance   = _____

4. in + ex + peri + ence + ed = _____

5. com + pete   = _____

6. com + pete + ite + ion   = _____

7. com + pete + ite + or   = _____

8. con + tinue + ous   = _____

F

Write the word for each meaning clue.

conscience   beneficial   immigrant   conscious   sandwich

1. someone who migrates into a country   _____

2. when your mind is awake   _____

3. a piece of meat between two slices of bread _____

4. something that is good for you   _____

5. the part of your mind that knows right from wrong _____

G

You learned that **q-u** pronounced "kw" works like two consonants. So a word like **quit** is actually is a short morphograph that ends **cvc**.

Add the morphographs together. Remember that **q-u** acts like two consonants when it sounds like "kw."

1. quit + er   = _____

2. e + quip + ment = _____

3. in + quire + y   = _____

4. quiz + ed   = _____

5. e + quip + ed   = _____

6. ac + quit + al   = _____

7. ac + quaint + ed = _____

8. quiet + ed   = _____

> Lesson 70 is a test lesson.
> There is no worksheet.

Lesson 71

A

continu<u>uous</u>   conspic<u>uous</u>   virt<u>uous</u>   strenuous   tenuous

B

1. spac_____   3. virt_____   5. grac_____
2. conspic_____   4. nutrit_____   6. malic_____

C

_____

D

1. _____
2. _____

E

Write the morphographs for each word. Remember to put a + between them.

1. compete _____
2. competition _____
3. vacuous _____
4. vacuum _____
5. equipment _____
6. equipped _____
7. comply _____
8. fortify _____

F

Find the seven misspelled words in the student's answer. Then write the words correctly.

Sometimes two different animals cooperate in a way that benefits both of them. When they do, their relationship is called commensalism. The relationship between the rhinoceros and a bird called a tick bird is a good example of commensalism. The rhinoceros has many annoying parasites living in the folds of its skin. These insects are a fine source of food for the tick bird, which makes its home on the rhino's back. The bird gets all the food it wants, and the rhino gets rid of annoying pests. A tick bird often lives its entire life on a rhino's back.

Explain the arrangement between the rhinoceros and the tick bird.

The tick bird is a bird that lives on the back of a rhinoseros. This resorseful bird eats the annoying ensects it finds in the folds of the rino's skin.

This relasionship benifits both the rhino and the tick bird. This arangement is called commensalism.

—————————————

—————————————

—————————————

—————————————

—————————————

—————————————

—————————————

Lesson 72

A

1. stren_____
2. grac_____
3. contin_____
4. consc_____
5. caut_____
6. cur_____

B

conquer   conquest   antique   acquaintance   quietly

C

_____

D

Make nine real words from the morphographs in the box.

quiz	quit	count	ac	ing	quire	ed

1. _____
2. _____
3. _____
4. _____
5. _____
6. _____
7. _____
8. _____
9. _____

Add the morphographs together.

1. multi + ply   = _____

2. re + fuse + ed   = _____

3. se + pare + ate + ion = _____

4. oc + cur + ed   = _____

5. in + di + vide + ual = _____

6. ex + peri + ence   = _____

7. e + vacu + ate   = _____

8. ap + ply + ing   = _____

If words with **q-u** make the sound "kw," they are from Latin. If they do not make the sound "kw," but make a sound like "koo" or "kur," they are not Latin words.

Write all the Latin words. Do not write any words that are not from Latin.

acquitted	conquest	acquaintance	inquiry
conquer	mosquito	quietly	

_____   _____   _____

_____   _____

Lesson 73

A

1. virt_____

2. luxur_____

3. ten_____

4. spac_____

5. conscient_____

6. vic_____

7. conspic_____

8. caut_____

B

1. _____

2. _____

C

Two words in this exercise have the morphograph **luxe.** The morphograph **luxe** means "fancy." Something that is deluxe is very fancy.

Add the morphographs together.

1. re + loco + ate = _____

2. suc + cess + ful = _____

3. loco + al = _____

4. ap + ply = _____

5. luxe + ury = _____

6. luxe + ury + ous = _____

7. ident + ify = _____

8. vice + ious + ness = _____

D

You know that some words can be spelled two ways, depending on where you live. **Program** and **programme** are two spellings of one word. **Centre** and **center** are two spellings of another word.

Most longer words containing **program** or **programme** have only one spelling. **Programming** is a correct spelling everywhere in the English-speaking world. Here's why the spelling is the same whether we start with **program** or **programme**.

The doubling rule applies to **pro + gram + ing = programming**.

The final-vowel rule applies to **pro + gramme + ing = programming**.

Most words built from **centre** and **center** have only one spelling. The reason is that all English-speaking people use the allomorph **centre** to make longer words, like **central** and **concentrate**.

Add the morphographs together.

1. centre + al   = _____

2. gramme + ar   = _____

3. gram + ar   = _____

4. con + centre + ate   = _____

5. ec + centre + ic   = _____

6. pro + gram + er   = _____

7. pro + gramme + er   = _____

8. de + centre + al + ize = _____

Lesson 74

A

1. _____
2. _____
3. _____
4. _____
5. _____
6. _____
7. _____
8. _____
9. _____
10. _____
11. _____
12. _____
13. _____

14. _____
15. _____
16. _____
17. _____
18. _____
19. _____
20. _____
21. _____
22. _____
23. _____
24. _____
25. _____

B

1. _____
2. _____

Write the correct spelling for each word. Then write one of these letters after each word:

Write **O** if the word is spelled by just putting the morphographs together.
Write **A** if the final-vowel rule explains why the spelling is changed.
Write **B** if the doubling rule explains why the spelling is changed.
Write **C** if the **y**-to-**i** rule explains why the spelling is changed.

		word	rule
1.	un + pro + tect + ed =	_____	_____
2.	com + pel + ing =	_____	_____
3.	de + luxe =	_____	_____
4.	dis + loco + ate =	_____	_____
5.	un + con + trol + able =	_____	_____
6.	con + sci + ous =	_____	_____
7.	e + quip + ment =	_____	_____
8.	con + centre + ate =	_____	_____

D

Three words in this exercise have the morphograph **tain.** In Latin **tain** means "to hold."
A container holds things.

Add the morphographs together.

1. pro + fess + ion = _____
2. per + tain + ing = _____
3. centre + al = _____
4. enter + tain = _____
5. cure + ious = _____
6. pro + ject + ion = _____
7. main + tain = _____
8. re + ject + ed = _____

> Lesson 75 is a test lesson.
> There is no worksheet.

Lesson 76

A

1. _____

2. _____

B

You know these words.

pear

weight

waist

These words sound the same.

pair: two

wait: not doing something yet

waste: things you throw away

Write the correct word for each sentence.

1. We bought apples and **pairs/pears.** _____

2. That belt won't fit around his **waist/waste.** _____

3. I'll **weight/wait** ten more minutes. _____

4. The **weight/wait** of the snow made the roof fall in. _____

5. Riki has a **pair/pear** of twin sisters. _____

6. Busy people don't like to **waist/waste** time. _____

C

Write the morphographs for each word. Remember to put a + between them.

1. weighed _____

2. weight _____

3. profess _____

4. presentation _____

5. affectionate _____

6. wasteful _____

7. experimental _____

8. absent _____

Find the misspelled words in these sentences. Then write the words correctly.

1. The experiment was a sucess. _____

2. We made to sandwitches. _____

3. They requirred more equipment. _____

4. Exercize can benifit your health. _____

Lesson 77

A

1. _____

2. _____

B

Write the correct word or words for each sentence.

1. She lost **weight/wait** around her **waste/waist**. _____

2. We have a peach tree and a **pair/pear** tree. _____

3. Some people **waste/waist** money on luxuries. _____

4. The train can't **weight/wait** any longer. _____

5. Kim bought a **pear/pair** of tickets. _____

C

Write the morphographs for each word. Remember to put a + between them.

1. waiter _____

2. unsuccessful _____

3. manually _____

4. wholesome _____

5. excessive _____

6. science _____

7. multiply _____

8. previous _____

Circle the misspelled word in each group. Then write it correctly.

1. identify	2. vacuum	3. wieghed	4. approach
pedel	expedient	previous	admire
museum	sandwich	experience	conshence
simplify	dipartment	radiate	luxury
_____	_____	_____	_____
5. perceive	6. equiped	7. conscious	8. acquainted
varyous	conquer	individuel	absent
pitying	acquittal	manifest	equal
fortieth	quiz	mystery	constent
_____	_____	_____	_____

Write the word for each meaning clue.

competitors   simplify   deluxe   challenge   pair

1. have a contest with   _____

2. other contestants   _____

3. make simple   _____

4. fancy   _____

5. two   _____

Lesson 78

poison<u>ous</u>   fam<u>ous</u>   joy<u>ous</u>   nervous   tremendous

B

Add the morphographs together.

1. loco + ate + ion   = _____
2. ap + ply + ance   = _____
3. story + es   = _____
4. ply + able   = _____
5. nerve + ous   = _____
6. treme + or   = _____
7. treme + end + ous   = _____
8. ident + ify + ing   = _____
9. leve + er   = _____
10. e + leve + ate + ion = _____

C

Many words in the English language end in the allomorph **er:** swimm**er,** bowl**er,** farm**er.**
The morphograph **er** means "one who." Here's a rule about most of those: they came after
the shorter word. The word **swim** came before the word **swimmer.**

The word **beggar** is different. It is spelled differently because it came about differently.
The word **beg** did not come into the language first. The word **beggar** came first. This
word came from a group of monks called **beggards.** The monks asked people on
the street for food. Their name was spelled **b-e-g-g-a-r-d,** so the word **beggar** is spelled
with the letters **a-r,** not **e-r.** The word **beg** came into the language later. **Beg** told what
beggars do. The word **beggar** is a single morphograph word.

Answer the items.

1. What does the morphograph **er** mean? _____

2. By the spelling of these words you can tell which word probably came first. Circle the words that came first.

    box, boxer   receive, receiver

    photograph, photographer   writer, write

    voter, vote   manage, manager

3. What are the morphographs in **swimmer?** _____

4. A **beggar** is one who begs. If **a-r** were a morphograph in the word **beggar,** what would it mean? _____

5. **A-r** is not a morphograph in **beggar.** How many morphographs is **beggar?** _____

D

A student wrote this letter. Eight words are misspelled. Write each of these words correctly.

Dear David,

Thank you for the lovely note you cent. I can't denie that I've weighted a long time to right you. I'm so absint-minded these days. I'm constintly forgeting things. In fact, I've forgotten why I'm writing you. My conscince has been telling me to write, so I have.

Love,
Sis

_____

_____

_____

_____

_____

_____

_____

Lesson 79

A

1. _____

2. _____

B

ridicul<u>ous</u>   synonym<u>ous</u>   numer<u>ous</u>   hazardous   famous

C

1. suspic_____   4. var_____   7. cur_____

2. fam_____   5. conspic_____   8. contin_____

3. consc_____   6. tremend_____

D

Add the morphographs together.

1. ridicule + ed   = _____

2. ridicule + ous   = _____

3. com + ply + ance = _____

4. numer + ic + al   = _____

5. numer + ous   = _____

6. marry + age   = _____

7. marry + ing   = _____

8. re + leve + ant   = _____

9. deny + al   = _____

10. beauty + ful   = _____

Write the morphographs for each word. Remember to put a **+** between them. Two of these words are single-morphograph words.

1. performance _____

2. proceeded _____

3. conceivable _____

4. varying _____

5. beggar _____

6. classifying _____

7. forgotten _____

8. experience _____

9. sandwich _____

10. pliable _____

In Lesson 81 you'll have a spelling contest. Some of the words below will be used in the contest.

equipped	resent	ridicule	creation
acquainted	luxury	pedal	disappoint
embarrass	advice	elevator	conquer

Lesson 80 is a test lesson.
There is no worksheet.

Lesson 81

A

Write the correct spelling for each word. Then write one of these letters after each word:

Write **O** if the word is spelled by just putting the morphographs together.
Write **A** if the final-vowel rule explains why the spelling is changed.
Write **B** if the doubling rule explains why the spelling is changed.
Write **C** if the **y**-to-**i** rule explains why the spelling is changed.

		word	rule
1.	myst + er + y + ous =	_____	_____
2.	ter + or =	_____	_____
3.	ter + ify + ing =	_____	_____
4.	ob + ject + ion + able =	_____	_____
5.	im + ply + ing =	_____	_____
6.	in + spect + ion =	_____	_____
7.	in + spect + or =	_____	_____
8.	hi + story =	_____	_____

B

Write the correct word for each sentence.

1. We found a **pair/pear** of shoes.   _____

2. The table could not support the **wait/weight.**   _____

3. She doesn't want to **waist/waste** any more time.   _____

C

Sometimes a longer word comes into the language first, and a shorter word comes later. An example is the word **beggar.** It is the longer word; it came first. The shorter word, **beg,** came later.

When the longer word comes first, we say the shorter word is a "back formation." Here's another example of back formation. The word **veterinarian** came into the language first. The word **vet** came later.

Answer the items.

1. The word **gymnasium** is a very old word. It comes from Greek. What shorter word later came from **gymnasium?** Write it. _____

2. The word **caravan** is a very old word. It is a group of people and their belongings that move like a train from place to place. A shorter word has come from the word **caravan.** It refers to something that moves from place to place. But this thing is a modern vehicle with an engine. Can you name it? _____

3. The words **examine** and **examination** are very old words. What shorter word means "an examination?" _____

Lesson 82

A

1. _____   6. _____
2. _____   7. _____
3. _____   8. _____
4. _____   9. _____
5. _____   10. _____

B

1. _____
2. _____

C

1. _____
2. _____

D

Add the morphographs together.

1. hurry + ing   = _____

2. friend + ly + ness   = _____

3. com + pete + ite + ion = _____

4. com + pete + ent   = _____

5. op + port + une + ity + es = _____

6. worry + ed   = _____

7. rob + er + y + es   = _____

8. un + deny + able   = _____

Answer the items.

1. The word **laboratory** is an old word. This word refers to a place   _____
   where you can make a careful study of things and how they work.
   A three-letter word later came from the longer word. Write that word.

2. The word **influenza** is an old word that refers to a sickness.   _____
   Influenza is a common sickness that many people seem to get
   at the same time. People have a fever; they cough, and they
   ache; their noses run. After a few days they get better, but this
   sickness may hang on for weeks. The word that you know for
   influenza came after the older word. The modern word is three
   letters long and begins with **f.** Write that word.

3. A **submarine** is a vehicle that can travel completely underwater.   _____
   A shorter word came after that word. The shorter word refers to
   the same vehicle. Write that word.

Five of these words are misspelled. Find the misspelled words. Then write them correctly.

1. wasteful
2. centril   _____
3. sandwich
4. beggar   _____
5. luxury
6. strenuus   _____
7. profession
8. obvius   _____
9. synonim
10. conquer   _____
11. varyous
12. clearance

Lesson 83

You know these words.

coarse
affect
site

These words sound the same.

course: a route or path you follow
effect: an outcome
sight: seeing

Write the correct word for each sentence.

1. The president will decide our next **coarse/course** of action. _____

2. Looking directly into the sun can harm your **site/sight**. _____

3. His yelling has a bad **affect/effect** on everyone around him. _____

4. We will build our house on that **site/sight**. _____

5. The storm will **affect/effect** traffic. _____

6. The wool is very **coarse/course**. _____

B

Add the morphographs together.

1. glory + ous   = _____

2. ab + rupt + ly   = _____

3. hi + story + an   = _____

4. for + ty + eth   = _____

5. con + tain + er   = _____

6. cor + rupt + ion   = _____

7. cor + rect + ly   = _____

8. multi + ply + ing   = _____

9. ter + ible   = _____

10. enter + tain + ment = _____

Find the ten misspelled words in the student's answer. Then write them correctly.

Chemicals that we use to control pests can affect other animals as well. Suppose a field is sprayed to kill insects. The mice that live in the field eat the plants that have been sprayed. After a few weeks, the mice will have eaten so much seed that they may contain a very high concentration of the spray chemical. When an eagle or a falcon eats one of these mice, the bird takes a large dose of the chemical. The bird may die or lay eggs with weak shells that could never hatch. In this way the poison becomes part of a natural food chain and affects every animal in the chain.

How might humans be affected by the poisons we use on pests?

People who use poison to controll pests don't realize that these dangerous cemichals can effect all animals, including humans. Anemals who eat poizoned insects probably won't die, but they may get weeker and their babyes may die. The meet we eat is at the end of the food chain, so it has had a chance to build up large consentrations of dangrous poisons.

_____

_____

_____

_____

_____

_____

_____

_____

_____

_____

Lesson 84

A

1. _____   4. _____

2. _____   5. _____

3. _____   6. _____

B

Write the correct word for each sentence.

1. I took my friend to the golf **coarse/course**.   _____

2. Oil spills can have a serious **affect/effect** on seagulls.   _____

3. This material is too **coarse/course** to wear next to my skin. _____

4. Seeing his friends again will probably **affect/effect** him.   _____

5. The church was rebuilt on the same **sight/site**.   _____

6. I can't see him anymore; he's out of **site/sight**.   _____

C

Words that end in consonant-and-**y** follow the final-vowel rule. The word **worry** ends consonant-and-**y**. When we add **ing,** we hear the sound for the **y** and the sound for the **i**. So we keep the letters for both sounds: **worrying.**

The word **glory** ends consonant-and-**y**. When we add **ify,** we do not hear the sound for the **y** and the sound for the **i**. So we drop the **y**. It does not change to **i**. Here's how we spell the word: **glorify.**

Say the word you get by combining **very + ify.** Does **very** end consonant-and-**y**? Do you hear the sound for both the **y** and the **i** in the combined word?

Say the word you get by combining **agony + ize.** Do you hear the sound for both the **y** and the **i**?

Remember this about words that end consonant-and-**y**. In words like **worrying, applying, studying, terrifying,** and **certifying,** you can hear both vowels, so we keep the **y.**

In words like **applicant, certificate, categorize, pacifist, historic,** and **terrific,** you cannot hear both vowels, so we drop the **y.**

Add the morphographs together.

1. beauty + ify   = _____

2. apply + ing   = _____

3. apply + icant = _____

4. certify + icate = _____

5. terrify + ic   = _____

6. agony + ize   = _____

7. history + ic   = _____

8. terrify + ing = _____

D

The morphograph **uni** means "one." Below are words that use the morphograph **uni.**

unite: When parts unite, they become one thing.

uniform: When individual people wear a uniform, they wear one outfit. Everybody wears the same thing.

union: A group of things that have become one is called a union.

unicycle: A unicycle is a vehicle with only one wheel.

Write the morphographs for each word.

1. _____ + _____ = uniform

2. _____ + ion = union

3. _____ + _____ = unicycle

4. _____ + ite = unite

Answer the item.

5. One vowel drops in the words **union** and **unite.** What vowel? _____

Write the correct words using **uni.**

6. All those players have the same _____.

7. The army and the air force will _____ forces.

8. The _____ of the two forces will make our country unbeatable.

9. Tina can ride a bicycle, but she can't ride a _____.

Lesson 85 is a test lesson.
There is no worksheet.

Lesson 86

A

1. _____

2. _____

B

You learned about dropping the final **y** from words that end in consonant-and-**y.** You drop the **y** when you can't hear it.

Combine the parts.

1. very + ify   = _____

2. spy + ing   = _____

3. certify + icate   = _____

4. deny + ing   = _____

5. justify + ication = _____

6. comply + icate   = _____

7. supply + ing   = _____

8. marry + ing   = _____

9. history + ic   = _____

10. category + ize   = _____

C

Write the morphographs for each word.

1. disruptive   _____

2. unaffected   _____

3. affection   _____

4. reunite   _____

5. effective   _____

6. effort   _____

7. fortify   _____

8. certify   _____

In Lesson 84 you learned that **uni** means "one." Here are other words that have the morphograph **uni**.

unique: Something that is one of a kind is unique.

unit: Whatever you count as one is a unit.

universe: The one thing that is in every direction you turn is the universe. It is so large that it is made of everything we know, all the stars, the planets, the sun, Earth—everything.

unison: When people speak in unison, they say the same thing at the same time. They speak as one person.

Write the morphographs for each word.

1. _____ + ique + _____ = uniqueness

2. _____ + _____ = universe

3. _____ + it = unit

4. _____ + _____ = unison

Answer the items.

5. One vowel drops in the words **unique** and **unit.** What vowel? _____

6. The morphograph **corn** means "horn." What do the morphographs in the word **unicorn** mean? _____

Write the correct words using **uni.**

7. The reason their team plays so well is that they all work together like a _____.

8. Everybody sang "Happy Birthday" in _____.

9. He looked up at the stars and said, "What a huge _____."

Lesson 87

A

1. _____   11. _____
2. _____   12. _____
3. _____   13. _____
4. _____   14. _____
5. _____   15. _____
6. _____   16. _____
7. _____   17. _____
8. _____   18. _____
9. _____   19. _____
10. _____   20. _____

B

1. _____
2. _____

C

You learned about dropping the final **y** from words that end in consonant-and-**y.** You drop the **y** when you can't hear it.

Combine the parts.

1. bury + ing   = _____

2. category + ize   = _____

3. glory + ify   = _____

4. terrify + ing   = _____

5. multiply + ication = _____

6. certify + ing   = _____

7. certify + icate   = _____

8. prehistory + ic   = _____

9. pacify + ing   = _____

10. pacify + ist   = _____

D

In Lessons 84 and 86, you learned that **uni** means "one." Here are other words that have the morphograph **uni.**

unify: Another way of saying that things unify is they unite or become one.

unity: Unity is another word for oneness.

unanimous: The morphograph **anima** means "spirit or life." When something is unanimous, everybody agrees. Everybody behaves as if they are one in spirit or belief.

Write the morphographs for each word.

1. _____ + ify = unify

2. _____ + _____ + ic + _____ + _____ = unification

3. _____ + anima + _____ = unanimous

4. _____ + ity = unity

Write the correct words using **uni.**

5. They are going to _____ the schools into one school district.

6. Since the team began to play like one single person, the team has a lot of

_____.

7. The decision to continue was _____.

Answer the items.

8. One vowel drops in the words **unite, unify, union, unit, unique,** and **unity.** What vowel?   _____

9. Two vowels drop in the word **unanimous.** Which vowels?   _____

10. Three vowels drop in the word **unification.** Which vowels?   _____

11. What does the morphograph **anima** mean?   _____

12. The word **animal** is frequently misspelled. You can see the morphograph **anima** in the word **animal.**
Combine the morphographs....**anima + al = ___.**   _____

Lesson 88

A

1. _____   3. _____

2. _____   4. _____

B

1. ten_____   5. hazard_____

2. prev_____   6. malic_____

3. unanim_____   7. suspic_____

4. caut_____   8. synonym_____

C

You have learned the word **unicycle** and what it means. A **unicycle** is a vehicle with only one wheel. The part of **unicycle** that you know is **uni.** That part means "one." The part that you don't know is **cycle.** You know that a unicycle has only one wheel. So you may be able to figure it out that **cycle** refers to something that goes around in a circle. Below are some words that use the morphograph **cycle.**

bicycle: The morphograph **bi** means "two." A bicycle is a vehicle with two wheels.

tricycle: The morphograph **tri** means "three." A tricycle is a vehicle with three wheels.

cyclone: A cyclone is a wind that goes around and around, like a wheel.

cyclic: Things that are cyclic follow the same pattern of a wheel that goes around and around. Cyclic things happen again and again.

bicyclist: The morphograph **ist** means "one who." A bicyclist is someone who rides a bicycle.

Write the morphographs for each word.

1. _____ + _____ = bicycle

2. _____ + one = cyclone

3. _____ + _____ = unicycle

4. _____ + _____ = tricycle

5. _____ + _____ = cyclic

6. _____ + _____ + _____ = bicyclist

Answer the items.

1. What does the morphograph **uni** mean? _____

2. What does the morphograph **bi** mean? _____

3. What does the morphograph **tri** mean? _____

4. How many angles does a **triangle** have? _____

5. Something that is **equilateral** has equal sides.
   If **lateral** refers to sides, what is the word for
   something that has two sides? _____

D

Find the misspelled words in these sentences. Then write the words correctly.

1. The beggor told numerrous tales. _____

2. Our acommodations were grasious and luxerious. _____

3. Each applycant recieved a questionaire. _____

4. The corupt rober did not have a guilty consciense. _____

E

Add the morphographs together.

1. uni + verse + al   = _____

2. re + verse + al   = _____

3. verse + ate + ile   = _____

4. poison + ous   = _____

5. ter + or   = _____

6. ridicule + ous   = _____

7. verse + ate + ile + ity = _____

© SRA/McGraw-Hill. All rights reserved.

Lesson 89

A

1. _____
2. _____
3. _____
4. _____

5. _____
6. _____
7. _____
8. _____

B

1. _____
2. _____
3. _____

C

Add the morphographs together.

1. caut + ion   = _____
2. caut + ious   = _____
3. ter + ify   = _____
4. super + flu + ous   = _____
5. uni + it   = _____
6. in + flu + ence   = _____
7. flu + id   = _____
8. hi + story + ic + al = _____

D

A student wrote this report. Nine words are misspelled. Write each of those words correctly.

At the last union meeting, we unanimusly voted to strike for higher wages. The workars in the bycicle dipartment will go on strike first. The people in the stuffed animel department will go on strike next. Since we will be striking right before the holidays, this will undenyably hurt busness, and we might have a better chance of getting our wages increased.

The next unyon meating will be held after work on Tuesday, November 18.

_____

_____

_____

_____

_____

_____

_____

_____

_____

E

Write the morphographs in each word.

1. experiment _____

2. interruption _____

3. fortunate _____

4. bicycle _____

5. universe _____

6. pleasant _____

7. competent _____

8. effortless _____

Lesson 90 is a test lesson.
There is no worksheet.

Lesson 91

A

You learned about dropping the final **y.** The only time you would ever drop the final **y** is when the next morphograph begins with **i** and you hear only one vowel sound. If the word ends consonant-and-**y** and the next morphograph begins with any letter but **i,** you never drop the **y.** You change the **y** to **i.**

When we combine **carry + age,** we cannot hear a sound for both the **y** and the **a.** We don't drop the **y** because the next morphograph does not begin with **i.** We just change the **y** to **i.**

When we combine **bury + ed,** we cannot hear a sound for the **y** and for the **e.** We don't drop the **y** because the next morphograph does not begin with **i.** We just change the **y** to **i.**

Add the morphographs together.

1. marry + age   = _____

2. glory + ous   = _____

3. glory + ify   = _____

4. busy + ness   = _____

5. study + es   = _____

6. ap + ply + ic + ant = _____

7. ap + ply + ing   = _____

8. hi + story + an   = _____

B

You know these words.

stationery
aisle
principal

These words sound the same.

stationary: can't move
isle: island
principle: rule

Write the correct word for each sentence.

1. The crew was shipwrecked on a desert **aisle/isle.** _____

2. The **principal/principle** gave a speech on the first day of school. _____

3. A horse stood **stationary/stationery** in the field, staring at the cowboy. _____

4. Our secretary has ordered more office _____
stationary/stationery.

5. The bride looked radiant as she walked down the **aisle/isle.** _____

6. It is against his **principals/principles** to cheat people. _____

C

Write the word for each meaning clue.

unique	beggar	bicycle	unite	cyclic

1. a person who asks for food _____

2. become one thing _____

3. when things happen again and again _____

4. a vehicle with two wheels _____

5. one of a kind _____

D

The allomorphs **judge** and **judice** mean "to judge." Here are some words that use the allomorphs **judge** and **judice.**

judicial: Something related to the courts or the law is judicial.

judicious: Someone who is wise (capable of good judgement) is judicious.

misjudge: When you make a bad estimate, you misjudge.

prejudge: When you judge something before you should, you prejudge it.

prejudice: An opinion formed without knowledge or reason is prejudice.

Note: In parts of the English-speaking world, **judge + ment** is spelled **judgement.** In the United States and parts of Canada, this word is often spelled **judgment.**

Write the morphographs for each word.

1. _____ + _____ + _____ = misjudged

2. _____ + _____ = prejudge

3. _____ + _____ = prejudice

4. _____ + ious = judicious

5. _____ + ial = judicial

6. _____ + _____ + _____ = prejudicial

Answer this item.

7. What is unusual about this spelling of **judge + ment = judgment?** _____

Write the correct words using **judge** or **judice.**

8. Only the most _____ men and women should be leaders.

9. A courtroom is where most _____ questions are answered.

10. A person with a strong _____ has a lot of hate.

11. I try not to _____ people I don't know very well.

12. We _____ how much cake to make for the party.

Lesson 92

A

1. _____

2. _____

B

Write the correct spelling for each word. Then write one of these letters after each word:

Write **O** if the word is spelled by just putting the morphographs together.
Write **A** if the final-vowel rule explains why the spelling is changed.
Write **C** if the **y**-to-**i** rule explains why the spelling is changed.

	word	rule
1. very + ify =	_____	_____
2. like + ly + hood =	_____	_____
3. marry + age =	_____	_____
4. com + ply + ing =	_____	_____
5. deny + ed =	_____	_____
6. just + ify + able =	_____	_____
7. agony + ize =	_____	_____
8. category + es =	_____	_____

C

Write the correct word for each sentence.

1. There were sales in every **aisle/isle**.   _____

2. Statues are **stationary/stationery**.   _____

3. Scientists must study the rules and **principals/principles**   _____
   of physics.

4. For our vacation, we stayed on an **aisle/isle** in the   _____
   South Pacific.

5. Mark was sent to the **principal/principle**.   _____

6. I need to buy more **stationary/stationery**.   _____

154 Lesson 92

D

Find the misspelled words in these sentences. Then write the words correctly.

1. He commited a terible crime. _____

2. The historean was very buzy. _____

3. All morphografs have meenings. _____

4. The magisian performed two uneque tricks. _____

E

Add the morphographs together.

1. anima + al   = _____

2. uni + anima + ous = _____

3. super + flu + ous = _____

4. judice + ious   = _____

5. flu + ent + ly   = _____

6. re + uni + ion   = _____

F

In the next lesson you'll have a spelling contest. The words below will be used in the contest.

animal	category	ridicule	influence
competent	versatile	identify	bicycle
carriage	caution	wasteful	business

Lesson 93

A

1. _____

2. _____

B

Write the correct spelling for each word. Then write one of these letters after each word:

Write **O** if the word is spelled by just putting the morphographs together.
Write **A** if the final-vowel rule explains why the spelling is changed.
Write **B** if the doubling rule explains why the spelling is changed.
Write **C** if the **y**-to-**i** rule explains why the spelling is changed.

	word	rule
1. uni + anima + ous =	_____	_____
2. marry + age =	_____	_____
3. pre + caut + ion =	_____	_____
4. patri + ot =	_____	_____
5. re + spect + able =	_____	_____
6. com + pany + es =	_____	_____
7. ter + ible =	_____	_____
8. sci + ent + ist =	_____	_____
9. sign + ify + ic + ant =	_____	_____
10. sci + ent + ify + ic =	_____	_____

C

Make twelve real words from the morphographs in the box.

| ident | uni | ed | ify | just | cert | very | ic | ate | ion |

1. _____   7. _____

2. _____   8. _____

3. _____   9. _____

4. _____   10. _____

5. _____   11. _____

6. _____   12. _____

D

Write the word for each meaning clue.

effect   affect   waist   waste   aisle   isle

sight   site   pair   pear   weight   wait

1. seeing _____

2. make it change _____

3. two _____

4. your midsection _____

5. measurement of heaviness _____

6. a row _____

7. an island _____

8. an outcome _____

9. a place _____

10. a certain fruit _____

11. not doing something yet _____

12. things you throw away _____

Lesson 94

A

1. _____

2. _____

B

1. _____ 5. _____

2. _____ 6. _____

3. _____ 7. _____

4. _____ 8. _____

C

Add these morphographs together.

1. com + pense + ate   = _____

2. ac + com + pany + ment = _____

3. in + sist + ent   = _____

4. con + sist + ence + y = _____

5. part + ial   = _____

6. in + flu + ent + ial   = _____

7. sub + sta + ant + ial = _____

8. re + spect + able   = _____

D

The morphograph **anti** means "against or opposite." Here are some words that use the morphograph **anti.**

antibody: An antibody is a cell that fights against disease in your body.

antonym: The morphograph **onym** means "name or word." Antonyms are words with the opposite meaning. Hot and cold are antonyms.

antisocial: Someone who doesn't like to be with people is antisocial.

antagonize: When you put somebody in agony or make that person mad, you antagonize the person.

antiperspirant: Something that fights perspiration is an antiperspirant.

158 Lesson 94

Write the morphographs for each word.

1. _____ + soci + _____ = antisocial

2. _____ + onym = antonym

3. _____ + _____ + _____ = antibodies

4. _____ + _____ + spire + _____ = antiperspirant

5. _____ + agony + _____ = antagonize

Answer the items.

6. It is easy to make words using **anti.** Make up a word that   _____
   means "against pollution." Make up a word that means
   "against war."

7. What does the morphograph **onym** mean?   _____

8. The word **anonymous** means "without a name." What does _____
   the morphograph **an** mean in the word **anonymous?**

9. One vowel drops in the word **antonym.** What vowel?   _____

10. Two vowels drop in the word **antagonize.** Which vowels?   _____

Write the correct words containing **anti.**

11. **Soft** and **easy** are both _____ of the word **hard.**

12. Many people have _____ that keep them well.

13. The hermit is so _____ that he won't even talk to people.

14. He is very malicious. He likes to _____ people.

Lesson 95 is a test lesson.
There is no worksheet.

Lesson 96

You know these words.

two
hole
weak

These words sound the same.

too: also
whole: entire
week: seven days

Write the correct word or words for each sentence.

1. Let Jim come **too/two.** _____

2. We worked all **weak/week** long. _____

3. She has **too/two** new puppies. _____

4. They buried the treasure in a **hole/whole** on the beach. _____

5. The girls ate **too/two hole/whole** pies. _____

6. His illness left him **weak/week** and shaky. _____

B

Add the morphographs together.

1. spire + it + ual = _____

2. per + sist + ent = _____

3. in + spire + ate + ion = _____

4. con + serve + ate + ion = _____

5. anti + onym = _____

6. philo + soph + ic + al = _____

7. in + sist + ed = _____

8. origin + ate = _____

9. in + spect + ion = _____

10. enter + tain + ment = _____

The morphograph **preci** means "price or value." This morphograph is always pronounced the same way, but its spelling works like the spelling of **sci.** The final vowel never drops. Below are some words that use the morphograph **preci.**

precious: Something very valuable is precious.

appreciate: When you recognize the value of something, you appreciate it.

depreciate: When the value of something decreases, it depreciates.

unappreciative: When you don't appreciate something, you are unappreciative.

Write the morphographs for each word.

1. _____ + _____ = precious

2. _____ + _____ + _____ = depreciate

3. _____ + _____ + _____ = appreciable

4. _____ + _____ + _____ = appreciate

5. _____ + _____ + _____ + _____ + _____ = unappreciative

Write the correct words using **preci.**

6. The _____ guest failed to thank his host for the excellent meal.

7. Some people don't _____ helpful criticism.

8. Diamonds and rubies are _____ stones.

9. If her house _____ any more, it will be completely worthless.

Lesson 97

A

Write the correct word or words for each sentence.

1. There's a **hole/whole** in this wall **too/two**. _____

2. The mansion took up the **hole/whole** block. _____

3. My sister likes her coffee **weak/week**. _____

4. Jim will leave in a **weak/week** or **too/two**. _____

B

If the morphograph **ex** is followed by a morphograph that begins with **s,** drop the **s.**

1. ex + sist   = _____

2. ex + cept   = _____

3. ex + spect   = _____

4. ex + ceed   = _____

5. ex + pense   = _____

6. ex + cite   = _____

7. ex + spire   = _____

8. ex + cel + ent = _____

C

Write the correct spelling for each word. Then write one of these letters after each word:

Write **O** if the word is spelled by just putting the morphographs together.
Write **A** if the final-vowel rule explains why the spelling is changed.
Write **B** if the doubling rule explains why the spelling is changed.
Write **C** if the **y**-to-**i** rule explains why the spelling is changed.

	word	rule
1. category + ize =	_____	_____
2. per + secu + ute =	_____	_____
3. com + pany + es =	_____	_____
4. con + secu + ute + ive =	_____	_____

		word	rule

5. be + gin + er = _____ _____

6. sign + ify + ic + ant = _____ _____

7. cert + ain = _____ _____

8. anti + onym = _____ _____

D

You may have learned that **motor** is a single-morphograph word. Actually it is made up of two morphographs—**mote** plus **or.** This passage tells more about the morphograph **mote.**

The morphograph **mote** means "to move." Here are some words that use the morphograph **mote.**

demote: When you move something to a lower position, you demote it.

remote: Something that is far away is remote.

promote: When you move something to a higher position, you promote it.

motion: Motion means movement.

motive: The reason for doing something is the motive.

Write the morphographs for each word.

1. _____ + _____ = motion

2. _____ + _____ = motive

3. _____ + _____ + _____ = automotive

4. _____ + _____ + _____ = promotion

5. _____ + _____ + _____ = commotion

6. _____ + _____ = motor

Write the correct words containing **mote.**

7. The blender won't run because the _____ is broken.

8. Good workers are _____.

9. The South Pole is the most _____ part of the world.

10. Hunger was the thief's _____ for stealing the bread.

11. The _____ of the waves sometimes makes people seasick.

Lesson 98

A

If the morphograph **ex** is followed by a morphograph that begins with **s,** drop the **s.**

1. ex + ceed   = _____

2. ex + spect   = _____

3. ex + cite   = _____

4. ex + port   = _____

5. ex + sist + ence = _____

6. ex + peri + ment = _____

7. ex + secu + ute = _____

8. ex + cel + ence = _____

B

Write the correct spelling for each word. Then write one of these letters after each word:

Write **O** if the word is spelled by just putting the morphographs together.
Write **A** if the final-vowel rule explains why the spelling is changed.
Write **B** if the doubling rule explains why the spelling is changed.
Write **C** if the **y**-to-**i** rule explains why the spelling is changed.

	word	rule
1. pro + mote + ion =	_____	_____
2. judice + ial =	_____	_____
3. pro + fess + ion + al =	_____	_____
4. hi + story + ic =	_____	_____
5. ex + cel + ent =	_____	_____
6. preci + ous =	_____	_____

For many words that have morphographs ending in the sound **d,** there is an allomorph that has an **s.** When we add the morphograph **ive** or **ion,** we use the allomorph with the **s.**

Here are some of those words. The second column shows the allomorph that comes before **ive** or **ion.**

comprehend	com + **prehense** + ion	= comprehension
explode	ex + **plose** + ive	= explosive
divide	di + **vise** + ion	= division
defend	de + **fense** + ive	= defensive

For each word below, write a real word that ends with the morphograph **ive.**

1. decide _____

2. persuade _____

3. offend _____

4. exclude _____

5. apprehend _____

6. include _____

7. expend _____

8. respond _____

A student wrote this letter. Ten words are misspelled. Write each of those words correctly.

Dear John,

    I'm so exsighted that you're coming to vizit us. Imajine, in just two weaks you'll be hear! I really appresiate the efort you're taking to come here. It will be so enjoiable to have companie.

See you soon,

J. J.

PS How do you like my new stationary?

_____

_____

_____

_____

_____

_____

_____

_____ _____ _____

Lesson 99

1. _____
2. _____
3. _____
4. _____
5. _____
6. _____
7. _____
8. _____
9. _____
10. _____

11. _____
12. _____
13. _____
14. _____
15. _____
16. _____
17. _____
18. _____
19. _____
20. _____

B

Add the morphographs together. Use your spelling rules.

1. ex + spire   = _____
2. ex + pand   = _____
3. ex + panse + ion   = _____
4. ex + cluse + ive   = _____
5. ex + peri + ence   = _____
6. ex + spect + ate + ion = _____
7. ex + secu + ute + ion = _____
8. ex + cess + ive   = _____

C

You have learned that many morphographs ending in a **d** sound have allomorphs that have an **s**. When we add **ive** or **ion,** we use the allomorph with the **s**. For each word below, write a real word that ends with the morphograph **ion.**

1. divide _____

2. comprehend _____

3. conclude _____

4. suspend _____

5. extend _____

6. erode _____

7. provide _____

8. invade _____

D

Write the word for each meaning clue.

judicious   too   antonym   motion   precious   whole

1. entire _____

2. a word with the opposite meaning _____

3. capable of good judgment _____

4. movement _____

5. also _____

6. something very valuable _____

Lesson 100 is a test lesson.
There is no worksheet.

Lesson 101

A

1. _____   4. _____

2. _____   5. _____

3. _____

B

When a word ends in the letters **a-g-e** and the next morphograph is **ous,** that part is spelled **a-g-e-o-u-s.** The final **e** is not dropped because the pronunciation of the **g** does not change. Remember how to spell the part that sounds like "age-us": **a-g-e-o-u-s.**

Add **ous** to these words. Remember that if the word ends in **a-g-e,** keep the final **e.**

Example: **outrage + ous = outrageous**

1. courage   _____

2. joy   _____

3. mystery   _____

4. advantage   _____

5. ridicule   _____

6. continue   _____

C

Make seven real words from the morphographs in the box.

in	ex	clude	con	spire	sist

1. _____   5. _____

2. _____   6. _____

3. _____   7. _____

4. _____

D

Some morphographs ending in the **f** sound are related to allomorphs that end in the **v** sound. By listening to the word, you can tell whether to use the allomorph with **f** or the allomorph with **v.**

Here are some words with allomorphs ending in the **f** sound.

grief	mischief	thief	fifty
relief	belief	twelfth	knife

Here are related words that end in the **v** sound.

grievance	mischievous	thievery	five
relieve	believe	twelve	knives

For each word below, write a word that has an **f** sound.

1. believe _____
2. mischievous _____
3. grieved _____
4. five _____

5. thieves _____
6. twelve _____
7. relieved _____
8. wives _____

E

Find the misspelled words in the sentences. Then write the words correctly.

1. Studyng sience is not a waist of time. _____
2. The questionnair was devided into four categoreys. _____
3. She is an inflooential exsecutive. _____
4. The dizaster effected the hole state. _____

Lesson 102

_____

Some words end with **ible.** Other words end with **able.** You can't tell which ending is used by the way the word is pronounced, and there is no rule that holds for all words. But there are some rules that will help you in most cases.

The ending we add to **nonwords** is usually **ible.** There are some exceptions, but here are some examples of nonwords that take **ible:**

incred + ible = incredible   poss + ible = possible
audi + ible = audible   suscept + ible = susceptible
hor + ible = horrible   transmiss + ible = transmissible
ter + ible = terrible   vise + ible = visible

The ending we add to most **words** is spelled **a-b-l-e.** There are exceptions to this rule too. But here are some words that follow the rule:

work + able = workable   predict + able = predictable
admire + able = admirable   excite + able = excitable

Some words that take **able** end in **g-e** or **c-e.** The final **e** doesn't drop in these words because the pronunciation is the same when we add **able.** So the **g** or the **c** must be followed by **e.** Here are some of those words:

change + able = changeable   notice + able = noticeable
manage + able = manageable   trace + able = traceable

1. permiss + able/ible   = _____

2. service + able/ible   = _____

3. poss + able/ible   = _____

4. conceive + able/ible   = _____

5. knowledge + able/ible = _____

6. compate + able/ible   = _____

7. charge + able/ible   = _____

8. consider + able/ible   = _____

C

Add **ous** to these words. Remember that if the word ends in **a-g-e,** keep the final **e.**

1. mystery _____
2. outrage _____
3. nerve _____
4. poison _____
5. courage _____
6. synonym _____
7. luxury _____
8. advantage _____

D

You have learned that some morphographs ending in the **f** sound have allomorphs that end in the **v** sound. By listening to the word, you can tell whether to use the allomorph with the **f** or with the **v.** For each word below, write a word that has a **v** sound.

1. relief _____
2. thief _____
3. belief _____
4. fifty _____
5. wolf _____
6. knife _____

Lesson 103

A

1. _____

2. _____

B

Write the correct spelling for each word. Then write one of these letters after each word:

Write **O** if the word is spelled by just putting the morphographs together.
Write **A** if the final-vowel rule explains why the spelling is changed.
Write **D** if the **ex** rule explains why the spelling is changed.

	word	**rule**
1. ex + spire =	_____	_____
2. ex + peri + ence =	_____	_____
3. di + vide + er =	_____	_____
4. ex + tract + ion =	_____	_____
5. pre + judice =	_____	_____
6. be + lieve + able =	_____	_____
7. per + secu + ute =	_____	_____
8. ex + sist + ence =	_____	_____

C

For some words that have a morphograph with a long-vowel sound there are related words that have short-vowel morphographs. The short-vowel morphograph is used when the word ends in **ion.** You can hear the difference in the sound of these morphographs.

explain	repeat	reveal	exclaim
explanation	repetition	revelation	exclamation

For each word below, write a real word that ends with **ion.**

1. explain _____

2. reveal _____

3. exclaim _____

4. repeat _____

You learned some general rules for using **able** and **ible**. The ending we add to words is usually **able**. The ending we add to nonwords is usually **ible**. Words that end **g-e** or **c-e** take **able** and do not drop the final **e**.

Write each word with the morphograph **able** or **ible**. Some morphographs have already been combined.

1. exchange + able/ible = _____

2. excite + able/ible = _____

3. suscept + able/ible = _____

4. poss + able/ible = _____

5. incride + able/ible = _____

6. trace + able/ible = _____

7. audi + able/ible = _____

8. manage + able/ible = _____

Lesson 104

Some words with more than one syllable end in the sound "eek." The ending of these words is spelled **i-q-u-e.** The reason is that we use the French spelling for these words, and the French spell "eek" with the letters **i-q-u-e.**

The word that sounds like "criteek" is spelled **c-r-i-t-i-q-u-e,** and the word that sounds like "misteek" is spelled **m-y-s-t-i-q-u-e.** Here are the rest of the "eek" words: techn**ique,** ant**ique,** phys**ique,** un**ique.**

These words are among the words most frequently misspelled. They are less difficult to spell if you remember that "eek" is spelled **i-q-u-e.**

B

You learned that some long-vowel morphographs have short-vowel allomorphs. The short-vowel allomorph is used when the word ends in **ion.**

For each word below, write a real word that ends in **ion.**

1. repeat _____

2. explain _____

3. reveal _____

4. proclaim _____

C

You learned some general rules for using **able** and **ible.** The ending we add to words is usually **able.** The ending we add to nonwords is usually **ible.** Words that end **g-e** or **c-e** take **able** and do not drop the final **e.**

Add the morphographs together. Choose **able** or **ible.** Use your spelling rules.

1. re + gret + able/ible = _____

2. just + ify + able/ible = _____

3. vise + able/ible = _____

4. note + ice + able/ible = _____

5. know + ledge + able/ible = _____

6. per + miss + able/ible = _____

7. ter + able/ible = _____

8. be + lieve + able/ible = _____

D

In Lesson 106 you'll have a spelling contest. Some of the words below will be used in the contest.

explain	manageable	courage	outrageous
explanation	relief	mystique	physique
technique	belief	repetition	decision

Lesson 105 is a test lesson.
There is no worksheet.

Lesson 106

A

The morphograph **soci** means "companion or friend." The morphograph is pronounced two different ways. The **c** sound makes the sound "sss" in some words and the sound "sh" in other words.

The spelling of **soci** works like the spelling of **sci** and **preci.** The final vowel never drops. Below are some words with the morphograph **soci.**

social: Things that are social involve having companions or friends.

society: A group of people who live and work together is called a society.

sociable: Someone who makes friends easily is sociable.

associate: When you put two things together, you associate them. Many people associate the flu with winter weather.

dissociate: When you separate two things, you dissociate them. He has dissociated himself from that gang of hoodlums. This word should not be spelled **disassociate.**

Write the morphographs for each word.

1. _____ + _____ + _____ = antisocial

2. _____ + _____ + _____ + _____ = association

3. _____ + _____ + _____ = dissociate

4. _____ + ety + _____ = societies

Answer the items.

5. Why does the word **associate** have two **s**'s? _____

6. What word means the opposite of **associate?** _____

Write the correct words containing **soci.**

7. Birds don't usually _____ with cats.

8. The Indians had the first known _____ in North America.

9. That hermit is so _____ that he hasn't spoken to anyone in ten years.

10. Several women formed a _____ club.

You already learned about the Greek morphographs for star: **aster** and **astro.** These allomorphs are in the words **astrology** and **disaster.**

The Latin morphograph for star is **sider.** The Romans were superstitious like the Greeks. They thought stars were involved in thinking. The word **consider** contains the Latin morphograph **sider.**

The French changed the Latin morphograph **sider** into **sire.** The French thought the stars had something to do with wishing for things. The word **desire** contains the French morphograph **sire.**

Write the morphographs for each word.

1. _____ + _____ = desire

2. _____ + _____ = consider

3. _____ + _____ + _____ + _____ = inconsiderate

4. _____ + _____ + _____ = desirable

5. _____ + _____ + _____ + _____ = consideration

6. _____ + _____ + _____ = desirous

7. _____ + _____ + _____ + _____ = undesirable

8. _____ + _____ + _____ + _____ = considerably

Write one of these meanings for each underlined word in the sentences.

      ill-starred event   wishes   thinks about

9. She <u>desires</u> to become famous.   _____

10. An earthquake is a natural <u>disaster</u>.   _____

11. Julie always <u>considers</u> all her choices before deciding.   _____

Write whether each morphograph is Greek, Latin, or French.

12. sider   _____

13. sire   _____

14. aster   _____

Lesson 107

A

1. _____

2. _____

B

The morphograph **fer** is in many words. It presents spelling problems because the **r** doubles for some endings but does not double for others. There's a simple way to tell whether the **r** in **fer** doubles: If the morphograph **fer** is stressed, or said loudly when you say the word, the **r** doubles. If **fer** is not stressed, the **r** does not double.

In these words the morphograph **fer** is stressed: **refer, confer, prefer.**
In these words the morphograph **fer** is not stressed: **offer, suffer, differ.**

When we add endings to words like **refer** and **confer,** the stress may change. If **fer** is no longer stressed in these words, the **r** does not double. In these words **fer** is not stressed: **reference, conference, preferable.** The **r** is not doubled in these words.

In these words **fer** is stressed, so the **r** is doubled: **conferred, referred, preferring.**

When you're adding the endings to a word that has the morphograph **fer,** say the word. If you stress **fer,** double the **r.** If you don't stress **fer,** do not double the **r.**

C

Some words that end in the sound "ur" are spelled with the letters **o-r** in the United States and are spelled with an **o-u-r** ending in the United Kingdom, Australia, and parts of Canada.

The U.S. spellings are **humor** and **labor;** the spellings in the United Kingdom and Australia are **humour** and **labour.**

Canada uses both spellings. Some people use the **o-r** spelling; others use the **o-u-r** spelling.

When you add **ize, ous,** or **ate** to any of these words that end with the sound "ur," the spelling is the same in all English-speaking countries. **Humorous** and **elaborate** are not spelled with **o-u-r,** even in England and Australia.

Add the morphographs to these words. Spell each word correctly.

1. vapor/vapour + ize = _____

2. glamor/glamour + ous = _____

3. labour/labor + ate + ory = _____

4. de + odor/odour + ize = _____

5. rigour/rigor+ ous = _____

6. glamor/glamour + ize = _____

7. e + vapor/vapour + ate = _____

8. humor/humour + ous = _____

D

There are two allomorphs for **9.** One is spelled **nine.** That morphograph is used in words like **nineteen.** The other allomorph is spelled **nin.** It always comes before **th.** The morphograph **nine** is used in all other words.

Here are words with the morphographs **nine** and **nin:**

ninety-five	twenty-ninth
nineteenth	ninth
ninetieth	forty-ninth

Write the word for each number.

Example: **90s = nineties**

19 = _____   90th = _____

9th = _____   99th = _____

Lesson 108

A

Some college-level words end in the morphographs **ane + ous.** When these morphographs are combined, do not drop the final **e.** Remember that the combined part is always spelled **a-n-e-o-u-s.**

Add **ous** to make words. Example: **extra + ane + ous = extraneous.** Remember to use your spelling rules.

1. simult + ane + ous = _____

2. miscell + ane + ous = _____

3. in + sta + ant + ane + ous = _____

4. spont + ane + ous = _____

B

You learned when the **r** in **fer** doubles. If **fer** is stressed in a word, the **r** doubles. If **fer** is not stressed, the **r** does not double.

Write the combined words.

1. of + fer + ed = _____

2. re + fer + ing = _____

3. in + fer + ing = _____

4. dif + fer + ent = _____

5. con + fer + ed = _____

6. suf + fer + ing = _____

7. re + fer + ed = _____

8. pre + fer + ence = _____

C

When you add a morphograph that begins with a vowel to some words that end in **e-r,** the final **e** drops. The following words end in **e-r.** They lose the final **e** when combined with morphographs that begin with **a, y,** or **o.**

anger	hunger	enter
disaster	register	administer
hinder	monster	wonder

© SRA/McGraw-Hill. All rights reserved.

Combine these morphographs that begin with **a, y,** and **o** with the words below.

1. anger + y   = _____

2. monster + ous   = _____

3. hinder + ance   = _____

4. register + ate + ion   = _____

5. wonder + ous   = _____

6. disaster + ous   = _____

7. hunger + y   = _____

8. administer + ate + ion = _____

9. enter + ance   = _____

D

Some words built from **labor** and **labour** are spelled the same everywhere in the English-speaking world. The reason is that everyone uses the allomorph **labor** to make longer words. **Labor** means "work."

Read the definitions; then complete the sentences.

elaborate: When you add more detail to something, you elaborate on that thing. Something that has a lot of detail is elaborate.

laborious: A task that requires a lot of hard work is a laborious task.

laboratory: A place where scientists work is a laboratory.

collaborate: When you work on a task with somebody else, you collaborate with that person.

1. Chopping firewood is a _____ job.

2. Clare and Pat are going to _____ on a book report.

3. Martin sewed an _____ design on his shirt.

4. Dr. Garcia keeps two hundred mice in her _____.

5. Can you _____ on your idea for saving money?

The morphograph **ity** at the end of a word like **humanity** or **formality** is an allomorph that is usually spelled **i-t-y.** In a few words, however, it is spelled **e-t-y.**

Here's the rule: When it follows a morphograph that ends in **y** or **i,** it is spelled **e-t-y.** When it follows any other letter, it is spelled **i-t-y.** You can hear the two vowel sounds when you use **ety.**

Write each word with the allomorph **ity** or **ety.** Use your spelling rules.

1. real + ity/ety   = _____

2. vary + ity/ety   = _____

3. soci + ity/ety   = _____

4. author + ity/ety = _____

5. propri + ity/ety = _____

6. anxi + ity/ety   = _____

Lesson 109

A

1. _____

2. _____

3. _____

B

You learned when the **r** in **fer** doubles. If **fer** is stressed in a word, the **r** doubles. If **fer** is not stressed, the **r** does not double.

Write the combined words.

1. pre + fer + ed   = _____

2. con + fer + ence = _____

3. dif + fer + ed   = _____

4. in + fer + ing   = _____

5. re + fer + ed   = _____

6. of + fer + ing   = _____

7. suf + fer + ed   = _____

8. re + fer + al   = _____

C

You have already learned that related words use the allomorphs **script** and **scribe.** When the word ends in **ion** or **ive,** the allomorph **script** is used.

There are other pairs of allomorphs that work the same way as **scribe** and **script.** Here they are:

sorb and **sorpt**   **duce** and **duct**   **sume** and **sumpt**

Here are examples of how the allomorphs are used:

pro**duce**   consume   ab**sorb**
pro**duct**ion   con**sumpt**ion   ab**sorpt**ion

For each word below, write a word that ends with **ion.**

1. introduce _____

2. assume _____

3. absorb _____

4. reduce _____

5. presume _____

6. deduce _____

D

These words lose the final **e** when combined with a morphograph that begins with **a, y,** or **o.**

Add the morphographs to these words. Be careful. The final **e** only drops when the next morphograph begins with **a, y,** or **o.**

1. hunger + y   = _____   6. enter + ance   = _____

2. disaster + ous = _____   7. wonder + ous = _____

3. disaster + s   = _____   8. wonder + ful = _____

4. monster + ous = _____   9. enter + y   = _____

5. hinder + ance = _____   10. enter + ed   = _____

E

Circle the misspelled word in each group. Then write it correctly.

1. possible
   considerable
   believible
   serviceable

   _____

2. nineteen
   ninety
   nineth
   forty-nine

   _____

3. sosiety
   personality
   variety
   identity

   _____

4. divide
   inspire
   dezire
   decision

   _____

5. expect
   exsist
   execute
   experiment

   _____

6. production
   consumption
   description
   repitition

   _____

Lesson 110 is a test lesson.
There is no worksheet.

184 Lesson 109

Lesson 111

A

1. _____

2. _____

3. _____

B

You learned that **nonwords** usually take the ending **ible,** not **able.**
There are exceptions. Here are the most important ones:

hospit + able = hospitable   ap + ply + ic + able = applicable
irrit + able = irritable   soci + able = sociable
capa + able = capable   ap + preci + able = appreciable

Here's a way to remember these exceptions. Nonwords like **hospit** and **applic** take other endings that begin with **a.**

For **hospit** there is **hospital.**   For **applic** there is **application** or **applicant.**
For **irrit** there is **irritate.**   For **soci** there is **social.**
For **capa** there is **capacity.**   For **appreci** there is **appreciate.**

Because **nonwords** like **hospit** and **applic** take one morphograph that begins
with **a,** they take the ending **able,** not **ible.**

If you want to test a nonword, see if you can make up a real word that takes one
of these endings: **al, ate, ation, ant,** or **acity.** If you can make up a word that takes
one of these endings, the nonword probably takes **able,** not **ible.**

For each word below, write a word that ends in **able** or **ible.**

1. social   _____

2. terrify   _____

3. serviced   _____

4. applicant   _____

5. duration   _____

6. capacity   _____

7. respected   _____

8. irritation   _____

9. hospital   _____

10. audience   _____

For each word below, write a real word that ends in **ion**. You will use allomorphs.
Example: **exclaim = exclamation**

1. divide _____

2. assume _____

3. deceive _____

4. introduce _____

5. explain _____

6. decide _____

7. reveal _____

8. absorb _____

You've learned allomorphs for **4, 5,** and **9.** The pairs of allomorphs are: **four, for; five, fif; nine, nin.**

Use the allomorphs to write the names of the numbers below.

4th = _____

50 = _____

95 = _____

44 = _____

19 = _____

9th = _____

In the next lesson you'll have a spelling contest. Some of the words below will be used in the contest.

hospital	relieve	disastrous	during
preference	irritable	possible	entrance

Lesson 112

A

Sometimes it is hard to tell the spelling of vowels near the end of the word. If you say the word **author** or **stupid,** you can't hear whether the letter before the final consonant should be **a, e, i, o,** or **u.** Here's a trick. If you can add the morphograph **ity** to the end of the word, the pronunciation changes. The pronunciation often makes it easier to hear which letter comes just before the final consonant.

When we add **ity** to **author,** we get the word **authority.** We can hear the **o** before the **r.** When we add **ity** to **stupid,** we get the word **stupidity.** We can hear the **i** sound before the **d.** When we add **ity** to **legal,** we get **legality.** We can hear the **a** sound before the **l.**

In the words below, there is a letter missing near the end of each word. That letter always makes a sound "uh."

Add **ity** to each word, and write the whole word with the correct spelling.
Example: **stup__d = stupidity**

1. pri__r   = _____

2. maj__r = _____

3. origin__l = _____

4. hum__d = _____

5. leg__l   = _____

B

For each word below, write a real word that ends in **ion.**

1. exclaim   _____

2. provide   _____

3. reduce   _____

4. perceive _____

5. prescribe _____

6. repeat   _____

7. produce _____

8. decide   _____

The spellings of many words tells us that the words went from Greek and Latin to French. There are different spellings of the **k** sound in Greek, Latin, and French. So we can tell the history of some words by looking at how the **k** sound is spelled.

If the **k** sound is spelled with the letters **ch,** the word originally came from Greek.

If the **k** sound is spelled with **c,** the spelling is Latin.

If the **k** sound is spelled with the letters **qu,** the spelling came from French.

The word **echo** has a **k** sound spelled with **ch,** so we use the Greek spelling for this word.

The word **captain** uses a **c** for the **k** sound. This word uses the Latin spelling of the **k** sound.

The word **technique** uses the letters **qu** for the **k** sound. This spelling comes from the French. (All the "eek" words spelled **ique** came from French.)

Some words with more than one **k** sound use different types of spelling for these sounds. The word **critique** has two **k** sounds. The first uses the Latin spelling. The second one uses the French spelling.

Words that use more than one spelling for the **k** sounds are among the most frequently misspelled words.

All the words below have two **k** sounds.

Underline the two **k** sounds in each word. Write the origin of the two **k** sounds on the lines. Here's an example: chronic: a. Greek b. Latin

1. technique: a. _____ b. _____

2. conquer: a. _____ b. _____

3. critique: a. _____ b. _____

4. chemical: a. _____ b. _____

Lesson 113

A

1. _____

2. _____

B

Remember that if a nonword takes one ending that begins with **a,** it will take **able,** not **ible.**

For each word below, write a word that ends in **able** or **ible.**

1. changed   _____

2. irritate   _____

3. permissive   _____

4. appreciate   _____

5. duration   _____

6. capacity   _____

7. considerate   _____

8. applicant   _____

C

Write the correct spelling for each word. Then write one of these letters after each word:

Write **O** if the word is spelled by just putting the morphographs together.
Write **B** if the **fer** doubling rule explains why the spelling is changed.

	word	rule
1. pre + fer + s =	_____	_____
2. pre + fer + ence =	_____	_____
3. in + fer + ed =	_____	_____
4. dif + fer + ent =	_____	_____
5. re + fer + ing =	_____	_____
6. suf + fer + ed =	_____	_____
7. con + fer + ed =	_____	_____
8. of + fer + ing =	_____	_____

The morphograph **loge** is very important. **Loge** comes from Greek, and it means "the word or name of something."

You have learned that **logic** is a single-morphograph word. Actually it is two morphographs—**loge** plus **ic**. When we combine these morphographs, the final **e** on **loge** drops, and we have the word **logic**.

Below are some other words that contain **loge**:

apologize = apo + loge + ize   analogy = ana + loge + y

Some words refer to the name of different studies. These words contain the morphograph **loge**:

Biology is the study of living things.

Astrology is the study of stars.

Geology is the study of the earth.

In all these words, the morphograph **loge** is followed by **y**. So the final **e** drops and the ending is spelled **logy.** These words tell the name for different studies.

Answer these items.

1. If **psycho** means "mind," what does the word **psychology** name?

   _____

2. If **entomo** means "insects," write the word that means "the study of insects."

   _____

3. If **anthropo** means "mankind," write the word that means "the study of mankind."

   _____

4. If **socio** means "a group of people," write the word that means "the study of people."

   _____

5. If **chrono** means "time," write the word that means "the study of time."

   _____

You learned a procedure for figuring out the vowel near the end of words. If you add the morphograph **ity** to the word, the pronunciation changes, and you may be able to hear the vowel sound.

In the words below, there is a letter missing near the end of each word. That letter always makes a sound "uh."

Add **ity** to each word, and write the whole word with the correct spelling.

Example: **leg__l = legality**

1. actu__l = _____

2. hospit__l = _____

3. stup__d = _____

4. hum__n = _____

5. pri__r = _____

Lesson 114

A

1. _____ 4. _____

2. _____ 5. _____

3. _____ 6. _____

B

Remember that if a nonword takes one ending that begins with **a,** it will take **able,** not **ible.**

For each word below, write a word that ends in **able** or **ible.**

1. hospitality
2. credit
3. capacity
4. vision

5. social
6. denial
7. audience
8. replacement

C

In Lesson 113 you learned that **loge** means "word or name." Many names of different studies contain **loge,** like the word **geology.**

Answer these items.

1. **Ornitho** means "bird." Write the word that means "the study of birds."

_____

2. **Morpho** means "form." Write the word that means "the study of forms."

_____

3. **Techno** means "skill." Write the word that means "the study of skills."

_____

4. **Theo** means "gods." Write the word that means "the study of gods, or religion."

D

The allomorphs **here** and **hese** mean "to stick." Here are some words that use **here** and **hese.**

adhere: To stick to something is to adhere to it.

adhesive: Something that sticks to things is adhesive.

cohesive: Things that stick together are cohesive.

coherent: When something makes sense, it is coherent.

hesitate: When something pauses, or sticks in time, it hesitates.

hesitant: Something that hesitates is hesitant.

192 Lesson 114

Write the morphographs for each word.

1. _____ + _____ + _____ = adhered

2. _____ + ite + _____ = hesitate

3. _____ + _____ + _____ + _____ = incoherent

4. _____ + _____ + _____ = hesitant

5. _____ + _____ + _____ = adherent

6. _____ + _____ + _____ = cohesive

An **e** or an **a** is missing from each word below. Write each word using the correct vowel.

7. hesit__nt   _____   9. hesit__ncy   _____

8. coher__nce   _____   10. adher__nt   _____

E

Find the ten misspelled words in the student's answer. Then write them correctly.

Mr. Mortenson was retired from his job as a construction contractor. He had made a lot of money, but he knew that many other people suffered because of extreme poverty. He decided to join with a group of people who built houses for people who could not afford to build a house of their own. The family that would live in the new house helped build it, so they really appreciated it. The people in the building group, however, helped themselves, not just the new home owners. They learned that they were happiest when they weren't greedy and selfish. They believed that selflessness was a benefit to everyone.

Describe Mr. Mortenson.

Mr. Mortenson was a retired construcsion contracter. _____
Although he had money, he knew that many peeple
suffered from poverty. He desided to help by building _____
houses for poor people. He beleived that selflessnes
benufited both the people who got the houses and the _____
people who built them. He was happyest when he was
unselfushly helping other people. The people who got _____
the new homes appreshiated them.

_____   _____

_____   _____

Lesson 115 is a test lesson.
There is no worksheet.

Lesson 116

A

1. _____   5. _____

2. _____   6. _____

3. _____   7. _____

4. _____   8. _____

B

In the words below, there is a letter missing near the end of each word. That letter always makes a sound "uh."

Add **ity** to each word, and write the whole word with the correct spelling.
Example: **person__l = personality**

1. re__l   =   _____

2. maj__r =   _____

3. leg__l =   _____

4. hum__d =   _____

5. auth__r =   _____

C

Write the morphographs for each word. Remember to put a + between them.

1. occur   _____

2. geologist   _____

3. biography   _____

4. biology   _____

5. apology   _____

6. changeable   _____

7. scientist   _____

8. conceivable _____

D

Words like **due** and **true** do not follow the final-**e** rule. When we add a morphograph that begins with a consonant to the end of these words, we drop the final **e**. Due + ly is spelled **duly. True + th** is spelled **truth.**

The strange spellings of these words came about because of something that happened about six hundred years ago. At that time, there were no printing presses. All books were written by people. The people who made copies of books were called scribes. For some reason scribes did not like words that end in **u** or **w.** Some words that they copied did end in **u** or **w.** At that time **due** was spelled **du,** and **true** was spelled **tru.** The scribes added the final **e** to these words. But the scribes did not add the final **e** to words like **truth** and **duty.**

So remember that words like **truth** and **duty** do not follow the final-**e** rule. These words are spelled as they used to be spelled. But **due** and **true** are newer spellings.

Add the morphographs together.

1. due + ly = _____

2. true + th = _____

3. due + ty = _____

4. true + ly = _____

The word **argue** used to be spelled **argu.** The word **awe** used to be spelled **aw.** The words below do not follow the final-**e** rule.

Add the morphographs together.

5. argue + ment = _____

6. awe + ful = _____

E

Make seven real words from the morphographs in the box. Use the **fer** doubling rule.

re	dif	fer	pre	ence	ed

1. _____

2. _____

3. _____

4. _____

5. _____

6. _____

7. _____

Lesson 117

A

1. _____

2. _____

3. _____

B

You have learned that adding **ity** can change the pronunciation of a word. Sometimes adding **ity** also changes the spelling. Here's how the spelling changes with **ous, able,** and **ible:**

ous + ity = osity   The **u** drops. You can hear the **o** sound in **osity.**
able + ity = ability   An **i** is added. You can hear it.
ible + ity = ibility   An **i** is added. You can hear it.

Add the morphograph **ity** to these words.

1. curious   _____

2. probable   _____

3. visible   _____

4. generous   _____

5. disable   _____

6. possible   _____

C

You learned about words like **truly** and **argument.** When we add a morphograph that begins with a consonant, we drop the final **e.**

Write the morphographs for each word.

1. _____ + th + _____ = truthful

2. _____ + ly = duly

3. _____ + ment = argument

4. _____ + ty = duty

5. _____ + ful + _____ = awfully

6. _____ +ly = truly

D

The word-history passage in Lesson 116 told about the scribes and how they changed the spellings of words that end in **u** or **w.** The scribes added a final **e** to these words. At the time there were other words, like **giv** and **hav.** These words were spelled the way they were pronounced. The scribes put an **e** on the end of them. But the pronunciation did not change. Today some words that end in **v-e** are spelled the way they sound: **save, stove.** Other words that end in **v-e** are not spelled the way they sound: **have, give.** Although these words follow the final-**e** rule, their pronunciation is strange.

Read the words below. In column one, write the words that are spelled the way they sound. If you say the letter name of the vowel in the middle of the word, write the word in column one. In column two, write the words that are not spelled the way they sound.

love	behave	glove
crave	have	hive
stove	give	

1   **2**

_____   _____

_____   _____

_____   _____

_____   _____

E

In the next lesson, you'll have a spelling contest. Some of the words below will be used in the contest.

irritate	behave	believe	biology
major	noticeable	technique	truly
ability	hesitate	argument	ninth

Lesson 118

A

Here's how the spelling changes when we add **ity** to **ous, able,** and **ible:**

ous + ity = osity	The **u** drops. You can hear the **o** sound in **osity.**
able + ity = ability	An **i** is added. You can hear it.
ible + ity = ibility	An **i** is added. You can hear it.

Add the morphograph **ity** to these words.

1. responsible _____

2. desirable _____

3. monstrous _____

4. durable _____

5. stable _____

6. compatible _____

B

Write the correct word or words for each sentence.

1. The **plain/plane** changed its **coarse/course**. _____

2. That equipment is not portable; it's **stationary/stationery**. _____

3. The suitcase blocked the **aisle/isle**. _____

4. The smog **affects/effects** my **sight/site**. _____

5. The garbage trucks take **waist/waste** to a disposal **sight/site**. _____

You learned that some words that end in **v-e** are spelled the way they sound: **save, stove.**
Other words that end in **v-e** are not spelled the way they sound: **have, give.** Although
these words follow the final-**e** rule, their pronunciation is strange.

Read the words below. In column one, write the words that are spelled the way they
sound. If you say the letter name of the vowel in the middle of the word, write the word in
column one. In column two, write the words that are not spelled the way they sound.

five	give	grave
save	have	move
love	cove	

1   **2**

_____   _____

_____   _____

_____   _____

_____   _____

Lesson 119

1. _____

2. _____

3. _____

B

The morphograph **ize** means "to make" or "to make more of something." **Ize** is used in words like **formalize, civilize, organize,** and **legalize.**

Ize is a very old morphograph that can be traced back to Latin and Greek words. The French also used this morphograph, but they changed the spelling to **ise.** Because some of our words come from Latin and others come from French, we have both **i-z-e** and **i-s-e** spellings in English.

Although both spellings are used in English, there is a rule for deciding whether the word is spelled with **ize** or **ise.** Here's the rule: Use **ize.**

This rule works for just about every word. Some words may be spelled with either **ise** or **ize.** For example, both **organize** and **organise** are acceptable spellings. For words that can be spelled both ways, the **ize** spelling is preferred.

Some words cannot be spelled both ways. Nearly all these end in **ize: computerize, modernize, legalize,** and many others. So if you use **ize,** you'll spell these words correctly.

By using **ize,** you'll spell thousands of words correctly. There are only two exceptions: **chastise,** which means "to scold," and **advertise.**

Combine the morphographs. Use **ise** only if you can't use **ize.**

1. ad + vert + ize/ise   = _____

2. organ + ize/ise + ate + ion = _____

3. critic + ize/ise   = _____

4. real + ize/ise   = _____

5. hospital + ize/ise   = _____

6. author + ize/ise + ate + ion = _____

You have learned that **nonwords** usually take the ending **ible** and that **words** usually take the ending **able.** You also learned that there are some **nonwords** that take **able. Able** is added to **nonwords** if there is a form of the word that ends in **al, ate,** or some other morphograph that begins with **a.**

Another group of exceptions is made of **words** that take **ible.** The words in this group are among the most frequently misspelled words. Even good spellers tend to add **able**—not **ible**—to words.

Here are some of the more important **words** that take **ible:**

force + ible = forcible
convert + ible = convertible
reduce + ible = reducible
reverse + ible = reversible
response + ible = responsible

corrupt + ible = corruptible
compress + ible = compressible
exhaust + ible = exhaustible
deduct + ible = deductible
resist + ible = resistible
sense + ible = sensible

For any words that take **ible,** there is a form of the word that ends in **ion** or **ive.** These morphographs begin with **i.**

For **exhaust** there is **exhaustive** or **exhaustion.**
For **deduct** there is **deductive** or **deduction.**
For **reverse** there is **reversion.**
For **corrupt** there is **corruption.**

For **compress** there is **compression.**
For **resist** there is **resistive.**
For **response** there is **responsive.**

Finding words that end in the morphograph **ion** or **ive** helps with some of the **ible** words. But it does not help with all of them. There is no rule for helping you spell **sensible,** and it is one of the most important words that end in **ible.** Study the **ible** words in the list above. Make sure that you know how to spell **sensible** and **responsible.** You will use these words frequently.

Write each word with the morphograph **able** or **ible.** Some morphographs have already been combined. Use your spelling rules.

1. response + able/ible   = _____

2. service + able/ible   = _____

3. applic + able/ible   = _____

4. invince + able/ible   = _____

5. sense + able/ible   = _____

6. ter + able/ible   = _____

7. irresponse + able/ible = _____

8. knowledge + able/ible = _____

D

The morphograph **vive** means "to live." Here are some words that use the morphograph **vive**.

survive: When you live through something, you survive it.

revive: When you bring something back to life, you revive it.

vivacious: Someone who is very lively is vivacious.

vivid: Something that is very bright and easy to see is vivid.

Write the morphographs for each word.

1. _____ + _____ + _____ = survivor

2. _____ + ace + _____ = vivacious

3. _____ + _____ + _____ = revival

4. _____ + id = vivid

5. _____ + _____ + _____ = survivable

Write the correct words using **vive**.

6. When he fainted, the nurse _____ him with smelling salts.

7. After the ship sank, one _____ drifted to an island.

8. The light was so _____ she had to close her eyes.

9. People always had a lot of fun when she was around because she was

   so _____.

> Lesson 120 is a test lesson.
> This is the last worksheet in Level F.

a	achieve		probably	actuality
	across		questionable	actually
	amusement		reestablish	radioactive
	amusing		regrettable	reaction
	arise		reliable	**ad** adequate
	around		replaceable	adhere
ab	abrupt		respectable	adhered
	abruptly		reusable	adherent
	absent		serviceable	adhesive
	absorbed		sociable	administration
	absorption		stability	admirable
able	ability		stable	admire
	admirable		survivable	admission
	applicable		traceable	admit
	appreciable		unbreakable	admittance
	believable		uncontrollable	admitted
	capability		undeniable	admitting
	capable		undeniably	advantage
	changeable		undesirable	advantageous
	chargeable		unforgettable	advertise
	conceivable		unjustifiable	advice
	considerable		unquestionable	advise
	considerably		usable	advised
	deniable		valuable	disadvantage
	desirability		variability	**af** affect
	desirable		variable	affected
	disability	**ac**	accommodate	affection
	durability		accommodation	affectionate
	durable		accommodations	affects
	enjoyable		accompaniment	affluent
	establish		accompany	unaffected
	establishment		account	**age** advantage
	exchangeable		accounted	advantageous
	excitable		accounting	baggage
	hospitable		acknowledge	carriage
	inconceivable		acknowledged	courage
	incurable		acquaintance	courageous
	indescribable		acquainted	disadvantage
	indispensable		acquire	encourage
	innumerable		acquired	encourage
	irritable		acquiring	encouraging
	justifiable		acquit	espionage
	knowledgeable		acquittal	leakage
	manageable		acquitted	leverage
	noticeable		acquitting	manage
	objectionable	**ace**	ace	manageable
	pliable		vivacious	managed
	portable	**ache**	backache	management
	predictable	**act**	action	manager
	predictably		actions	managerial
	preferable		activity	marriage
	probability		actor	mismanage

mismanaged
package
passage
patronage
storage
usage

agony
agonize
agony
antagonize

ain
captain
certain

air
airport

aire
questionnaire

al
acquittal
allocate
allotment
allotted
allowed
animal
animals
antisocial
astronomical
athletically
autobiographical
burial
central
chemical
chemicals
commensalism
critical
critically
decentralize
deferral
denial
departmental
equal
equalize
equally
experimental
fatal
final
finally
formal
graphically
historical
hospital
hospitality
hospitalize
hospitalized
hymnal
hysterical
ideal

impersonal
industrial
informal
legality
local
localize
magical
manual
manually
mechanical
mistrial
mystical
noncommittal
numeral
numerical
occasional
occasionally
original
originality
pedal
personal
personality
personalize
personalized
philosophical
physical
physically
principal
professional
punctual
quizzical
radial
referral
refusal
reversal
revival
rhetorical
rhythmical
sentimental
signal
social
socialize
spiral
trial
trivial
universal
unoriginal

example example
an anonymous
another
historian
humanity

ance
acquaintance
admittance
appearance
appliance
clearance
compliance
disappearance
distance
distances
endurance
entrance
grievance
hesitancy
hindrance
importance
performance
performances
relevance
remittance
vacancy
variance

anchor anchored
ane extraneous
instantaneous
miscellaneous
simultaneous
spontaneous

anger anger
angry

anima animal
animals
unanimous
unanimously

answer answer
ant antiperspirant
applicant
constant
constantly
equidistant
hesitant
immigrant
immigrants
important
instant
instantaneous
irrelevant
malignant
migrant
migrants
militant
pleasant
radiant

Word Parts

relevant
resistant
significant
substantial
unpleasant
vacant

ante antecedent
antique

anti antagonize
antibodies
antibody
antiperspirant
antisocial
antonym

anxi anxiety
anxious

ap appear
appearance
appeared
appearing
appliance
applicable
applicant
application
applied
apply
applying
appreciable
appreciate
appreciation
apprehensive
approach
approached
disappear
disappearance
disappeared
disappearing
disappoint
disappointed
unappreciative

apo apologize
apologized
apology
apostrophe

ar arrangement
familiar
familiarize
summarization
summarize
summary

arch patriarch

argue argue

argument

art art

ary contrary
dictionaries
dictionary
disciplinary
imaginary
military
stationary

as associate
association
assumed
assumption
fantasies
fantastic
fantasy
whereas

aster asterisk
disaster
disasters
disastrous

astro astrologer
astrology
astronaut
astronomer
astronomers
astronomical
astronomy

ate accommodate
accommodation
accommodations
adequate
administration
affectionate
allocate
application
appreciate
appreciation
associate
association
authorization
calculations
certificate
certification
characterization
citation
civilization
classification
collaborate
compensate
complicate
concentrate

concentration
concentrations
conservation
consideration
conversation
depreciate
depreciates
depreciation
deviate
deviation
dictate
dictation
dictator
dislocate
dissociate
duration
educate
educator
elaborate
elevation
elevator
emigrate
emigrated
enumerate
equate
equation
equator
evacuate
evacuated
exclamation
expectation
explanation
fortunate
hesitate
hyphenated
identification
imagination
imaginations
imaginative
immigrate
impersonate
inconsiderate
information
informative
infuriate
inspiration
irritate
irritated
justification
laboratory
locate
location

	manifestation		audition		benefit
	manipulate		auditor		benefits
	migrate	**author**	authority		benevolent
	migration		authorization		benign
	migratory		authorize	**bi**	bicycle
	moderate	**auto**	autobiographer		bicyclist
	moderator		autobiographical	**biblio**	bibliography
	multiplication		autobiography	**bid**	bidden
	observation		autograph		forbid
	organization		autographs		forbidden
	originate		automotive	**big**	biggest
	originator	**awe**	awe	**bio**	autobiographical
	presentation		awful		autobiography
	proclamation		awfully		biography
	pulsate	**baby**	babies		biology
	punctuate	**back**	backache	**blame**	blameless
	punctuation	**bag**	baggage	**body**	antibodies
	quotation		bagged		antibody
	radiate		bagging	**box**	boxer
	radiation	**bake**	baker	**boy**	boyish
	radiator		bakers	**break**	unbreakable
	registration		bakes	**breath**	breath
	relocate		baking		breathless
	reservation	**bank**	bankrupt		breathlessness
	respiration	**bare**	barely	**breathe**	breathe
	revelation	**base**	basement	**bridge**	bridge
	rheumatism		basic	**brother**	brother
	schematic	**be**	begin	**build**	build
	separate		beginner		building
	separation		beginning	**bury**	burial
	sophisticated		behave		buried
	state		behind		bury
	statement		belief		burying
	station		believable	**busy**	busily
	stationery		believe		business
	summarization		believed		businesses
	summation		believer		busy
	unappreciative		believes	**calcule**	calculations
	unfortunate		believing	**capa**	capability
	unfortunately		disbelief		capable
	unification	**beam**	beam	**car**	car
	vacate	**beauty**	beautiful	**care**	careless
	vacation		beautify	**carry**	carriage
	verification	**beggar**	beggar		carrier
	versatile	**bel**	bellicose		carries
	versatility		belligerent		carrying
athlete	athlete		rebel	**case**	casual
	athletic		rebellion		casually
	athletically		rebels		casualty
	athletics	**bene**	benediction		occasion
audi	audience		benefactor		occasional
	audible		beneficial		occasionally

Word Parts

	occasions		concentration	**ciple**	disciple
category	categories		decentralize		disciplinary
	categorize		eccentric		discipline
	category	**cept**	conception		principles
caught	caught		deception	**circle**	semicircle
caut	caution		deceptive	**cise**	decision
	cautious		except		decisive
	precaution		misconception		exercise
cede	antecedent		perception		exercises
	concede		perceptive		exercising
	conceded		preconception	**cite**	citation
	concedes		reception		excitable
	conceding		receptive		excite
	interceded		susceptible		excited
	precede	**ceros**	rhinoceros	**civil**	civil
	preceded	**cert**	certain		civilian
	precedence		certificate		civilization
	precedent		certification		civilize
	preceding		certified	**claim**	exclaim
	procedure		certify	**clame**	exclamation
	recede		certifying		proclamation
	receding		concert	**class**	classification
ceed	exceed		disconcert		classified
	exceeded	**cess**	excessive		classify
	exceeding		excessively		classifying
	exceedingly		process	**clear**	clearance
	proceed		success	**close**	close
	proceeded		successful		closed
	proceeding		unsuccessful		enclosure
	proceedings	**challenge**	challenge	**cloth**	cloth
	proceeds		challenged	**clothe**	clothe
	succeed	**change**	changeable		clothes
	succeeded		changing	**cloud**	cloudy
	succeeding		exchangeable	**clude**	conclude
ceive	conceivable	**character**	character		exclude
	deceive		characteristic		include
	deceived		characterization	**cluse**	conclusion
	deceiving		characterize		conclusions
	inconceivable	**charge**	chargeable		conclusive
	misconceive	**chaste**	chastise		exclusion
	perceive	**cheme**	chemical		exclusive
	perceived		chemicals		inclusive
	receive		chemistry	**co**	coherence
	received	**chief**	mischief		coherent
	receiver	**chieve**	achieve		cohesive
	receiving		mischievous		incoherent
cel	excel	**choly**	melancholy	**coarse**	coarse
	excelled	**chord**	chords		coarsely
	excellence	**chore**	chorus	**col**	collaborate
	excellent	**cide**	decide		collection
centre	central		decided	**colon**	colony
	concentrate	**cipe**	principal		semicolon

Word Parts

com	accommodate		conception		discontent
	accommodation		concert		discontinue
	accommodations		conclude		inconceivable
	accompaniment		conclusion		inconsiderate
	accompany		conclusions		inconsistent
	commensalism		conclusive		misconceive
	commit		concur		misconception
	commitment		concurred		preconception
	committed		concurrence		unconscious
	committee		concurrent		uncontrollable
	commodity		concurs	**contra**	contradict
	commotion		conductor		contradicted
	companies		confer		contradiction
	companion		conference		contradicts
	company		conferred		contrary
	compare		confined	**copy**	copied
	compatibility		confusing		copying
	compatible		confusion	**cor**	correctly
	compelled		conquer		corrupt
	compelling		conquest		corruptible
	compensate		conscience		corruption
	compete		conscientious	**cosmo**	cosmonaut
	competent		conscious	**count**	account
	competition		consecutive		accounted
	competitor		consents		accounting
	competitors		conservation	**could**	could
	completely		consider	**cour**	courage
	compliance		considerable		courageous
	complicate		considerably		encourage
	complied		consideration		encouraging
	comply		consist	**cove**	cove
	complying		consisted	**cover**	covered
	comprehension		consistency		discovered
	compress		consistent		discoveries
	compressible		conspicuous		recovered
	compression		conspire		uncover
	compromise		constant		undiscovered
	computer		constantly	**crave**	crave
	noncommittal		consumption	**crease**	increases
	recommend		contain	**create**	create
	recommended		contained		created
come	coming		container		creation
	welcome		continue		creator
comma	comma		continued		creature
con	concede		continuous	**crede**	credible
	conceded		control		credit
	concedes		controlled		incredible
	conceding		controlling	**critic**	critic
	conceivable		conversation		critical
	concentrate		converse		critically
	concentration		convertible		criticism
	concentrations		convince		criticize

Word Parts

critique critique

cross across

cry cried
crier
cry
crying

cur concur
concurred
concurrence
concurrent
concurs
currency
current
currently
curtail
occur
occurred
occurrence
occurrences
occurs
recur
recurred
recurrence
recurrences
recurrent
recurring
recurs

cure curiosity
curious
incurable
manicure
pedicure

cycle bicycle
bicyclist
cyclic
cyclone
tricycle
unicycle

danger dangerous

day day

de deceive
deceived
deceiving
decentralize
deception
deceptive
decide
decided
decision
decisive
deduct
deductible

deduction
deductive
defer
deferral
define
defined
definite
definitely
definition
deject
deluxe
demote
department
departmental
deport
deported
depreciate
depreciates
depreciation
describe
describes
descript
description
descriptive
desirability
desirable
desire
desirous
despise
destroyed
deter
deviate
deviation
devise
indefinite
indefinitely
indescribable
undefined
undesirable

dense density

deny deniable
denial
denied
deny
denying
undeniable
undeniably

di direct
direction
directly
distance
distances

divide
divided
divider
divisible
division
equidistant
individual

dict benediction
contradict
contradicted
contradiction
contradicts
dictate
dictation
dictator
diction
dictionaries
dictionary
edict
indict
indicted
indictment
malediction
predict
predictable
predictably
predicting
prediction

dif differ
differed
difference
different

dis disability
disadvantage
disappear
disappearance
disappeared
disappearing
disappoint
disappointed
disaster
disasters
disastrous
disbelief
disciple
disciplinary
discipline
discontent
discontinue
discovered
discoveries
disease

	diseased		equipped		forgiven
	dislocate		erosion		forgotten
	dispel		eruption		forsaken
	disruptive		espionage		given
	dissent		establish		gotten
	dissociate		establishment		happen
	indispensable		evacuate		happens
	undiscovered		evacuated		hidden
drive	driver		event		mistaken
	drivers		eventual		taken
	drives		reestablish		unenlightened
	driving	**each**	each	**ence**	audience
dry	drying	**early**	earlier		coherence
duce	educate		earliest		concurrence
	educator	**earn**	earn		conference
	introduce	**ease**	disease		conscience
	introduced		diseased		consistency
	produced		easier		currency
	reduced		easiest		difference
	reducible		easy		equivalence
duct	conductor	**eat**	eating		excellence
	deduct	**ec**	eccentric		existence
	deductible	**echo**	echo		experience
	deduction		echoes		inexperienced
	deductive	**eco**	economic		inference
	introduction	**ee**	committee		influence
	production	**ef**	effect		influenced
	reduction		effective		occurrence
	viaduct		effectively		occurrences
due	due		effort		precedence
	duly		effortless		preference
	duty	**el**	model		recurrence
Dutch	Dutch		personnel		recurrences
dure	durability	**embarrass**	embarrass		reference
	durable		embarrassed		science
	duration		embarrasses		sentence
	during		embarrassment		sentenced
	endurance	**en**	bidden	**end**	horrendous
	endure		enclosure		stupendous
	endured		encourage		tremendous
	enduring		encouraging	**ent**	adherent
e	edict		endurance		affluent
	educate		endure		antecedent
	educator		endured		belligerent
	elaborate		enduring		benevolent
	elevation		enjoy		coherent
	elevator		enjoyable		competent
	emigrate		enjoyed		concurrent
	emigrated		enjoyment		conscientious
	enumerate		enlightening		consistent
	equip		flatten		current
	equipment		forbidden		currently

Word Parts

	different		driver			washer
	equivalent		drivers			waxier
	excellent		earlier			weaker
	expedient		easier			wittier
	fluent		entertainer			wolverine
	fluently		exercise			worker
	incoherent		exercises			workers
	inconsistent		exercising			wrapper
	influential		geographer			wrappers
	insistent		happier			writer
	malevolent		healthier	**ern**		modern
	nonexistent		hindrance			modernize
	nutrient		lever	**est**		biggest
	persistent		luckier			driest
	precedent		manager			earliest
	recurrent		managerial			easiest
	repellent		manufacturer			fanciest
	residents		misnomer			friendliest
	scientific		moderate			greatest
	scientist		moderator			happiest
enter	entered		mysterious			heaviest
	enterprise		mysteriously			hottest
	entertain		mystery			interest
	entertainer		noisier			interesting
	entertainment		performer			luckiest
	entrance		photographer			modest
	entry		player			modestly
equi	adequate		porter			modesty
	equal		prayer			nastiest
	equalize		propeller			saddest
	equally		quitter			sorest
	equate		receiver			strangest
	equation		reporter			sturdiest
	equator		reviewer			sunniest
	equidistant		revolver			waxiest
	equinox		robber			whitest
	equivalence		robberies			widest
	equivalent		runner			wittiest
er	astrologer		sadder	**eth**		fortieth
	astronomer		server			ninetieth
	astronomers		shipper	**ety**		anxiety
	baker		shopper			propriety
	bakers		shoppers			societies
	beginner		sorer			society
	believer		stationery			variety
	belligerent		stranger	**ever**		every
	boxer		sunnier			whatever
	carrier		swimmer			whatsoever
	computer		swimmers			whoever
	container		thievery			whomever
	crier		voter	**ex**		example
	divider		waiter			exceed

exceeded		exports		different
exceeding		expressive		ferry
exceedingly		extension		infer
excel		extraction		inference
excelled		extractor		inferred
excellence		inexperienced		inferring
excellent		nonexistent		offer
except	**exam**	exam		offered
excessive	**extra**	extraneous		offering
excessively	**face**	surface		prefer
exchangeable		surfaced		preferable
excitable	**fact**	benefactor		preference
excite		factories		preferred
excited		manufacture		preferring
exclaim		manufacturer		prefers
exclamation	**fail**	failure		refer
exclude	**false**	falsify		reference
exclusion	**fame**	famous		referral
exclusive	**family**	familiar		referred
execute		familiarize		referring
execution		family		suffer
executive	**fancy**	fanciest		suffered
exercise		fancy		suffering
exercises	**fant**	fantasies		transfer
exercising		fantastic		transferred
exhaust		fantasy	**fess**	profess
exhaustible	**farm**	farming		profession
exhaustion	**fat**	fatty		professional
exhaustive	**fate**	fatal	**fest**	manifestation
exist	**fect**	affect	**fice**	beneficial
existence		affected		office
exit		affection		official
expand		affectionate		sacrifice
expansion		affects		sacrificial
expect		effect	**fif**	fifteen
expectation		effective		fifth
expecting		effectively		fifties
expedient		infection		fifty
expedite		perfect	**find**	find
expedition		unaffected		findings
expeditious	**fend**	defend	**fine**	confined
expend		offend		define
expense	**fense**	defensive		defined
expenses		offensive		definite
expensive	**fer**	confer		definitely
experience		conference		definition
experiment		conferred		final
experimental		defer		finally
expire		deferral		fined
explain		differ		finish
explanation		differed		finite
export		difference		indefinite

	indefinitely		reformed			refused
	infinite		transform	**gave**	gave
	infinitely		transformed	**gener**	generosity
	refining		uniform		generous
	undefined		uninformed	**geo**	geographer
fit	benefit	**fort**	effort		geographic
	benefits		effortless		geography
five	five		fort		geologist
	ninety-five		fortify		geology
fix	prefix		fortunate	**get**	forget
	unfixed		fortune		forgetting
flat	flatten		misfortune		unforgettable
flu	affluent		unfortunate	**gin**	begin
	flu		unfortunately		beginner
	fluent	**four**	forty-four		beginning
	fluently		four	**give**	forgive
	fluid		fours		forgiven
	influence		fourteen		forgiveness
	influenced		fourteenth		give
	influential		fourth		given
	influenza		ninety-fourth	**glory**	glorified
	superfluous	**friend**	friend		glorify
for	forbid		friendliest		glorious
	forbidden		friendliness	**glove**	glove
	forgetting		friendly	**got**	forgot
	forgive		friends		forgotten
	forgiven	**ful**	awful		gotten
	forgiveness		awfully	**grace**	grace
	forgot		beautiful		gracious
	forgotten		helpful		graciousness
	forsake		hopeful	**graph**	autobiographer
	forsaken		hopefully		autobiographical
	forties		joyful		autobiography
	fortieth		pitiful		autograph
	forty		playful		autographs
	forty-four		regretful		bibliography
	forty-ninth		resourceful		biography
	unforgettable		successful		geographer
force	forcible		thoughtful		geographic
form	formal		truthful		geography
	formless		unsuccessful		graph
	inform		useful		graphic
	informal		wasteful		graphically
	information		wonderful		graphics
	informative	**fun**	funny		graphite
	informing	**fury**	furious		graphs
	misinformed		fury		morphograph
	performance		infuriate		morphographs
	performances	**fuse**	confusing		paragraph
	performed		confusion		phonograph
	performer		refusal		photograph
	performing		refuse		photographer

Word Parts

photographic
photographs
photography
telegraph
grave grave
great great
greatest
greatly
gret regret
regretful
regrettable
grief grief
grieve grievance
grieved
grow growth
gym gym
hap haphazard
happen
happens
happier
happiest
happily
happiness
happy
mishap
mishaps
perhaps
unhappy
hard hard
hat hats
haust exhaust
exhaustible
exhaustion
exhaustive
have behave
have
hazard haphazard
hazardous
hazards
heal health
healthier
healthy
unhealthy
heavy heaviest
heaviness
help helpful
here adhere
adhered
adherent
coherence
coherent
incoherent

hese adhesive
cohesive
hesitancy
hesitant
hesitate
hi historian
historic
historical
history
prehistoric
hid hidden
hind behind
hindrance
hive hive
hood likelihood
hop hop
hopped
hope hope
hopeful
hopefully
hopeless
hopelessly
hoping
hor horrendous
horrible
horrid
horrify
hospit hospitable
hospital
hospitality
hospitalize
hospitalized
hot hottest
house warehouses
hume humanity
humidity
hunger hunger
hungry
hurry hurried
hurrying
hymn hymn
hymnal
hyphen hyphen
hyphenated
hyster hysterical
ial beneficial
impartial
influential
judicial
managerial
official
partial

partially
prejudicial
sacrificial
ian civilian
magician
musician
pedestrian
physician
ible audible
compatibility
compatible
compressible
convertible
corruptible
credible
deductible
divisible
exhaustible
forcible
horrible
incredible
invincible
invisible
irresponsible
legible
permissible
possibility
possible
reducible
resistible
responsibility
responsible
reversible
sensible
susceptible
transmissible
terrible
visibility
visible
ic applicable
applicant
application
astronomical
athletic
athletically
athletics
autobiographical
basic
bellicose
certificate
certification
characteristic

chemical
chemicals
classification
complicate
cyclic
eccentric
economic
geographic
graphic
graphically
graphics
historic
historical
hysterical
identification
justification
logic
mechanic
mechanical
mechanics
multiplication
music
musician
mystical
numerical
patriotic
philosophical
photographic
prehistoric
quizzical
replica
rhetoric
rhetorical
rhythmic
rhythmical
schematic
scientific
significant
sophisticated
symbolic
terrific
unification
verification

ice   justice
malice
malicious
notice
noticeable
service
serviceable
simplicity
unnoticed

id   fluid
horrid
humidity
stupid
stupidity
valid
vivid

idea   ideal

ident   identical
identification
identified
identify
identifying
identity

ify   beautify
certificate
certification
certified
certify
certifying
classification
classified
classify
classifying
falsify
fortify
glorified
glorify
horrify
identification
identified
identify
identifying
intensify
justifiable
justification
justified
justify
modify
mystify
pacifist
pacifying
personify
qualify
scientific
significant
signify
simplified
simplify
simplifying
terrific
terrify

terrifying
unification
unified
unify
unjustifiable
verification
verified
verify

ign   benign
malignant

il   peril

ile   versatile
versatility

im   immigrant
immigrants
immigrate
impartial
impediment
impersonal
impersonate
implying
import
importance
important
imported
importing
improved
improvement
improving

image   imaginary
imagination
imaginations
imaginative
imagine

in   include
inclusive
incoherent
inconceivable
inconsiderate
inconsistent
increases
incredible
incurable
indefinite
indefinitely
indescribable
indict
indicted
indictment
indispensable
individual
inexperienced

	infection	imaginary	consideration
	infer	imagination	consumption
	inference	imaginations	contradiction
	inferred	imaginative	conversation
	inferring	imagine	corruption
	infinite	medicine	creation
	infinitely	wolverine	deception
	influence	**inter** interceded	decision
	influenced	interest	deduction
	influential	interesting	definition
	influenza	intermission	depreciation
	inform	interrupt	description
	informal	interruption	deviation
	information	**intro** introduce	dictation
	informative	introduced	diction
	informing	introduction	dictionaries
	infuriate	**ion** audition	dictionary
	injection	absorption	direction
	innumerable	accommodation	division
	inquire	accommodations	duration
	inquired	action	elevation
	inquiries	actions	equation
	inquiring	administration	erosion
	inquiry	admission	eruption
	inquisitive	affection	exclamation
	insects	affectionate	exclusion
	insist	application	execution
	insisted	appreciation	exhaustion
	insistent	association	expansion
	inspect	assumption	expectation
	inspection	authorization	expedition
	inspector	benediction	explanation
	inspiration	calculations	extension
	inspire	caution	extraction
	instant	certification	identification
	instantaneous	characterization	imagination
	instructor	citation	imaginations
	intensify	civilization	infection
	invasion	classification	information
	invent	collection	injection
	inversion	commotion	inspection
	invincible	companion	inspiration
	invisible	competition	intermission
	involvement	comprehension	interruption
	misinformed	compression	introduction
	twin	concentration	invasion
	twins	concentrations	inversion
	uninformed	conception	justification
industry	industrial	conclusion	location
	industry	conclusions	malediction
ine	disciplinary	confusion	manifestation
	discipline	conservation	migration

Word Parts

misconception
motion
multiplication
nutrition
objectionable
observation
occasion
occasional
occasionally
occasions
organization
perception
permission
persuasion
precaution
preconception
prediction
prescription
presentation
presumption
proclamation
production
profession
professional
projection
promotion
provision
punctuation
question
questionable
questioned
questionnaire
questions
quotation
radiation
reaction
rebellion
reception
reduction
registration
rejection
relationship
repetition
reservation
respiration
reunion
revelation
reversion
revision
separation
station
stationery

subscription
summarization
summation
supervision
suspension
television
translation
transmission
unification
union
unquestionable
vacation
verification
version
vision

ious
cautious
conscientious
curiosity
curious
expeditious
gracious
graciousness
judicious
laborious
malicious
nutritious
sacrilegious
spacious
suspicious
vicious
viciousness
vivacious

ique
antique
mystique
technique
unique
uniqueness

ir
irrelevant
irresponsible

irrit
irritable
irritate
irritated

ise
advertise
chastise

ish
boyish
establish
establishment
finish
reestablish
selfishness

isk
asterisk

isle
isle

island
ism
criticism
mechanism
rheumatism
ist
bicyclist
characteristic
chemistry
geologist
pacifist
physicist
scientist
sophisticated
it
auditor
credit
exit
spirit
spiritual
summit
transit
unit
visit
visitor
visitors
ite
competition
competitor
competitors
definite
definitely
definition
expedite
expedition
expeditious
finite
graphite
hesitancy
hesitant
hesitate
indefinite
indefinitely
infinite
infinitely
inquisitive
nutrition
nutritious
opposite
repetition
reunite
unite
united
veritable
ity
ability
activity

Word Parts

	actuality		exclusive		symbolize
	authority		execute	**ject**	deject
	capability		exhaustive		injection
	commodity		expensive		object
	compatibility		expressive		objected
	curiosity		imaginative		objectionable
	density		inclusive		objective
	desirability		informative		project
	disability		inquisitive		projection
	durability		locomotive		projector
	generosity		motive		rejected
	hospitality		objective		rejection
	humanity		offensive		subject
	humidity		perceptive	**joy**	enjoy
	identity		persuasive		enjoyable
	legality		prescriptive		enjoyed
	majority		radioactive		enjoyment
	monstrosity		receptive		joyful
	opportunities		resistive		joyous
	opportunity		responsive	**judge**	judging
	originality		submissive		misjudge
	personality		unappreciative		misjudged
	possibility	**ize**	agonize		prejudge
	priority		antagonize	**judice**	judicial
	probability		apologize		judicious
	quality		apologized		prejudice
	quantity		authorization		prejudicial
	reality		authorize	**juice**	juice
	responsibility		categorize	**just**	justice
	simplicity		characterization		justifiable
	stability		characterize		justification
	stupidity		civilization		justified
	unity		civilize		justify
	variability		criticize		unjustifiable
	versatility		decentralize	**knife**	knife
	visibility		equalize	**knive**	knives
ive	activity		familiarize	**knot**	knots
	adhesive		hospitalize		knotted
	apprehensive		hospitalized	**know**	acknowledge
	automotive		localize		acknowledged
	cohesive		mechanize		knowledge
	conclusive		memorize		knowledgeable
	consecutive		modernize	**lab**	lab
	deceptive		organization	**labor**	collaborate
	decisive		patronize		elaborate
	deductive		patronizes		laboratory
	descriptive		personalize		laborious
	disruptive		personalized	**lack**	lack
	effective		realize	**late**	lately
	effectively		socialize		relationship
	excessive		summarization		translate
	excessively		summarize		translation

Word Parts

lay	relay		listings		directly
leak	leakage	**lit**	litter		duly
	leaked	**loco**	allocate		effectively
	leaking		dislocate		equally
lect	collection		local		exceedingly
ledge	acknowledge		localize		excessively
	acknowledged		locate		finally
	knowledge		location		fluently
	knowledgeable		locomotive		friendliest
lege	legality		relocate		friendliness
	legible	**loge**	apologize		friendly
	sacrilege		apologized		graphically
	sacrilegious		apology		greatly
length	lengthy		astrologer		happily
less	blameless		astrology		hopefully
	breathless		biology		hopelessly
	breathlessness		geologist		indefinitely
	careless		geology		infinitely
	effortless		logic		lately
	formless		morphology		likelihood
	hopeless		ornithology		likely
	hopelessly		psychology		loneliness
	meaningless		radiology		lovely
	spotless		technology		manly
	starless		theology		manually
	valueless	**lone**	lone		modestly
leve	elevation		loneliness		mysteriously
	elevator	**lot**	allotment		obviously
	irrelevant		allotted		occasionally
	lever	**love**	love		partially
	relevance		lovely		physically
	relevant	**low**	allowed		quietly
lief	belief	**luck**	luckier		really
	disbelief		luckiest		sadly
	relief		lucky		sorely
lieve	believable	**luxe**	deluxe		strangely
	believe		luxurious		thoroughly
	believed		luxury		truly
	believer	**ly**	abruptly		unanimously
	believes		actually		unfortunately
	believing		athletically		unusually
	relieve		awfully		yearly
	relieved		barely	**mad**	madness
	relieves		busily	**magic**	magic
light	enlightening		casually		magical
	unenlightened		coarsely		magician
like	like		completely	**main**	maintain
	likelihood		constantly	**major**	major
	likely		correctly		majority
	likeness		critically	**male**	malady
lique	oblique		currently		malediction
list	list		definitely		malevolent

	malice		equipment		mistake
	malicious		establishment		mistaken
	malignant		experiment		mistakes
man	manly		experimental		mistral
mani	manicure		impediment	**miscell**	miscellaneous
	manifestation		improvement	**mise**	compromise
	manipulate		indictment	**miss**	admission
manu	manage		involvement		intermission
	manageable		management		omissions
	managed		movement		permissible
	management		nutriment		permission
	manager		replacement		submissive
	managerial		requirement		transmissible
	manual		resentment		transmission
	manually		sacrament	**mit**	admit
	manufacture		sentimental		admittance
	manufacturer		shipment		admitted
	manuscript		statement		admitting
	mismanage	**migra**	emigrant		commit
	mismanaged		emigrate		commitment
many	many		emigrated		committed
marry	marriage		immigrant		committee
	married		immigrants		noncommittal
	marry		immigrate		omit
	marrying		immigration		omitted
	remarried		migrant		permit
mean	meaningless		migrants		permitted
	meanings		migrate		permitting
	meant		migration		remittance
mechan	mechanic		migratory		submit
	mechanical	**milit**	militant		submitted
	mechanics		military		transmit
	mechanism	**minister**	administration		transmitting
	mechanize	**mire**	admirable	**mode**	accommodate
medic	medicine		admire		accommodation
meet	meeting	**mis**	mischief		accommodations
melan	melancholy		mischievous		commodity
meme	memorize		misconceive		mode
mend	recommend		misconception		model
	recommendation		misfortune		moderate
	recommended		mishap		moderation
ment	allotment		mishaps		moderator
	amusement		misinformed		modern
	argument		misjudge		modernize
	arrangement		misjudged		modest
	basement		mismanage		modestly
	commitment		mismanaged		modesty
	department		misnomer		modify
	departmental		misplaced	**monster**	monster
	embarrassment		misspell		monstrosity
	enjoyment		misspelling		monstrous
	entertainment		misspells	**morpho**	morphograph

	morphographs	**nice**	nice		occurs
	morphology	**nin**	forty-ninth	**of**	offensive
mote	automotive		ninety-ninth		offer
	commotion		ninth		offered
	demote	**nine**	nineteen		offering
	locomotive		ninetieth		office
	motion		ninety		official
	motive		ninety-five	**on**	espionage
	motor		ninety-fourth		patron
	promoted		ninety-ninth		patronage
	promotion	**noise**	noise		patronize
	promoter		noisier		patronizes
	remote		noisy	**one**	cyclone
move	move	**nome**	astronomer	**onym**	anonymous
	movement		astronomers		antonym
multi	multiplication		astronomical		synonym
	multiply		astronomy		synonymous
	multiplying		economic	**op**	opportune
muse	amusement		misnomer		opportunities
	amusing	**non**	noncommittal		opportunity
	museum		nonexistent		opposite
	music	**note**	notice	**or**	actor
	musician		noticeable		auditor
myst	mysterious		unnoticed		benefactor
	mysteriously	**nox**	equinox		competitor
	mystery	**numer**	enumerate		competitors
	mystical		innumerable		conductor
	mystify		numeral		creator
	mystique		numerical		dictator
nasty	nastiest		numerous		educator
	nasty	**nutri**	nutrient		elevator
naut	astronaut		nutriment		equator
	cosmonaut		nutrition		extractor
nerve	nervous		nutritious		factories
ness	breathlessness	**o**	omissions		inspector
	business		omit		instructor
	businesses		omitted		memorize
	forgiveness	**ob**	object		moderator
	friendliness		objected		motor
	graciousness		objectionable		originator
	happiness		objective		projector
	heaviness		observation		promoter
	likeness		obvious		radiator
	loneliness		obviously		supervisor
	madness	**oc**	occasion		survivor
	sadness		occasional		terror
	selfishness		occasionally		tremor
	soreness		occasions		visitor
	strangeness		occur		visitors
	uniqueness		occurred	**organ**	organization
	viciousness		occurrence	**origin**	origin
new	new		occurrences		original

	originality
	originally
	originate
	originator
	unoriginal
ornitho	ornithology
ory	laboratory
	migratory
ot	patriot
	patriotic
	patriots
other	another
our	our
ous	advantageous
	anonymous
	anxious
	conscious
	continuous
	courageous
	dangerous
	desirous
	disastrous
	extraneous
	famous
	furious
	generosity
	generous
	glorious
	hazardous
	horrendous
	instantaneous
	joyous
	luxurious
	miscellaneous
	mischievous
	monstrosity
	monstrous
	mysterious
	mysteriously
	nervous
	numerous
	obvious
	obviously
	outrageous
	poisonous
	precious
	previous
	ridiculous
	simultaneous
	spontaneous
	strenuous
	stupendous

	superfluous
	synonymous
	tremendous
	unanimous
	unanimously
	unconscious
	vacuous
	various
	virtuous
	wondrous
out	outrage
	outrageous
paci	pacifist
	pacifying
pack	package
	packed
	packing
pand	expand
panse	expansion
pany	accompaniment
	accompany
	companies
	companion
	company
para	paragraph
pare	compare
	prepared
	separate
	separation
part	department
	departmental
	impartial
	partial
	partially
	parting
pass	passage
	passed
	passport
pat	patting
pate	compatibility
	compatible
patri	patriarch
	patriot
	patriotic
	patriots
	patron
	patronage
	patronize
	patronizes
pear	appear
	appearance
	appeared

	appearing
	disappear
	disappearance
	disappeared
	disappearing
	pear
	pears
peat	repeat
pedi	expedient
	expedite
	expedition
	expeditious
	impediment
	pedal
	pedestrian
	pedicure
pel	compelled
	compelling
	dispel
	propel
	propeller
	propelling
	repel
	repelled
	repellent
pend	expend
	suspend
pense	compensate
	expense
	expenses
	expensive
	indispensable
	suspension
people	people
per	antiperspirant
	perceive
	perceived
	perception
	perceptive
	perfect
	performance
	performances
	performed
	performer
	performing
	perhaps
	permissible
	permission
	permit
	permitted
	permitting
	persecute

	persistent		replacement		exports
	persuade		replacing		import
	persuasion	**plain**	explain		importance
	persuasive	**plan**	plan		important
	pertaining		planned		imported
peri	experience		planning		importing
	experiment		plans		opportune
	experimental		unplanned		opportunities
	inexperienced	**plane**	explanation		opportunity
	peril	**plant**	plants		passport
period	period		transplant		port
person	impersonal	**play**	play		portable
	impersonate		played		porter
	personal		player		report
	personality		playful		reported
	personalize	**please**	pleasant		reporter
	personalized		pleasure		reports
	personify		unpleasant		support
	personnel	**plete**	completely		supported
pete	compete	**plot**	plotted		transport
	competent	**ply**	appliance		transporting
	competition		applicable		unreported
	competitor		applicant	**pose**	opposite
	competitors		application		suppose
	repetition		applied	**poss**	possibility
philo	philosophical		apply		possible
	philosopher		applying	**pray**	prayer
	philosophy		compliance	**pre**	precaution
phone	symphony		complicate		precede
	telephone		complied		preceded
phono	phonograph		comply		precedence
photo	photograph		complying		precedent
	photographer		implying		preceding
	photographic		multiplication		preconception
	photographs		multiply		predict
	photography		multiplying		predictable
phrase	phrase		pliable		predictably
	rephrase		replica		predicting
	rephrased		replied		prediction
physic	physical		supplies		prefer
	physically		supplying		preferable
	physician	**point**	disappoint		preference
	physicist		disappointed		preferred
	physics	**poison**	poison		preferring
physique	physique		poisoned		prefers
picnic	picnic		poisoning		prefix
pity	pitiful		poisonous		prehistoric
	pity	**police**	police		prejudge
place	misplaced	**port**	airport		prejudice
	place		deport		prejudicial
	placing		deported		prepared
	replaceable		export		prescribe

	prescription		propelling	**quise**	required
	prescriptive		prosecute	**quit**	requirement
	present		protected		inquisitive
	presentation		provision		acquit
	presented		unprotected		acquittal
	presumption	**proach**	approach		acquitted
	previewing		approached		acquitting
	previous	**probe**	probability		quitter
preci	appreciable		probably		quitting
	appreciate	**propi**	propriety	**quiz**	quiz
	appreciation	**prove**	improved		quizzed
	depreciate		improvement		quizzes
	depreciates		improving		quizzical
	depreciation	**psycho**	psychology		quizzing
	precious	**pule**	manipulate	**quote**	quotation
	unappreciative	**pulse**	pulsate		quote
prehend	apprehend	**punctu**	punctual		quoted
	comprehend		punctuate	**race**	race
prehense	apprehensive		punctuation		racing
	comprehension		puncture	**radio**	radial
press	compress	**pute**	computer		radiant
	compressible	**quaint**	acquaintance		radiate
	compression		acquainted		radiation
	expressive	**quale**	qualify		radiator
	pressure		quality		radioactive
prin	principal	**quant**	quantity		radiology
	principles	**quer**	conquer	**rage**	outrage
prior	priority	**quere**	queries		outrageous
prise	enterprise		query	**rain**	raining
	surprise	**quest**	conquest	**range**	arrangement
pro	compromise		question	**re**	irrelevant
	procedure		questionable		irresponsible
	proceed		questioned		reaction
	proceeded		questionnaire		rebel
	proceeding		questions		rebellion
	proceedings		request		rebels
	proceeds		unquestionable		recede
	process	**quiet**	quieted		receding
	proclamation		quieter		receive
	produced		quietly		received
	production	**quip**	equip		receiver
	profess		equipment		receiving
	profession		equipped		reception
	professional	**quire**	acquire		receptive
	project		acquired		recommend
	projection		acquiring		recommended
	projector		inquire		recovered
	promoted		inquired		recur
	promotion		inquiries		recurred
	promoter		inquiring		recurrence
	propel		inquiry		recurrences
	propeller		require		recurrent

recurring
recurs
reduced
reducible
reduction
reestablish
refer
reference
referral
referred
referring
refining
reformed
refusal
refuse
refused
regretful
regrettable
rejected
rejection
relationship
relay
relevance
relevant
relief
relieve
relieved
relieves
relocate
remarried
remittance
remote
repeat
repel
repelled
repellent
repetition
rephrase
rephrased
replaceable
replacement
replacing
replica
report
reported
reporter
reports
request
require
required
requirement
resent

resentment
reservation
residents
resist
resistant
resisted
resistible
resistive
resourceful
respect
respectable
respiration
response
responsibility
responsible
responsive
reunion
reunite
reusable
revelation
reversal
reverse
reversible
reversion
reviewer
revised
revision
revival
revived
revolve
revolver
unreported

real real
reality
realize
really

rect correctly
direct
direction
directly

register register
registration

rely reliable
rest rest
rhetor rhetoric
rhetorical
rheum rheumatism
rhino rhino
rhinoceros
rhinorrhea
rhyme rhyme
rhymed

rhyming
rhythm rhythm
rhythmic
rhythmical
ridicule ridicule
ridiculed
ridiculous
rise arise
rob robber
robberies
rode erode
rose erosion
rough rough
round around
surrounding
rrhea rhinorrhea
run runner
running
runny
rupt abrupt
abruptly
bankrupt
corrupt
corruptible
corruption
disruptive
eruption
interrupt
interruption
rupture
ry chemistry
sacra sacrament
sacri sacred
sacrifice
sacrificial
sacrilege
sacrilegious
sad sadder
saddest
sadly
sadness
safe safety
sake forsake
forsaken
sample sampled
sandal sandal
sandwich sandwich
sandwiches
save save
say saying
says
scheme schematic

Word Parts

	scheme	**serve**	conservation		resist
	scheming		observation		resistant
school	school		reservation		resisted
	schooling		server		resistible
sci	conscience		service		resistive
	conscientious		serviceable	**sit**	sitting
	conscious	**shine**	shiny	**skin**	skinny
	science	**ship**	relationship	**slam**	slammed
	scientific		ship	**snap**	snap
	scientist		shipment		snapped
	unconscious		shipper	**so**	whatsoever
scope	telescope		shipping	**soci**	antisocial
scribe	describable	**shop**	shopper		associate
	describe		shoppers		association
	describes		shopping		dissociate
	prescribe		shops		sociable
	subscribe	**should**	should		social
script	descript	**show**	showed		socialize
	description		shows		societies
	descriptive	**side**	residents		society
	manuscript	**sider**	consider	**some**	wholesome
	prescription		considerable		worrisome
	prescriptive		considerably	**son**	unison
	subscription		consideration	**soph**	philosophical
	transcript		inconsiderate		philosophy
se	separate	**sign**	signal		sophisticated
	separation		signed	**sorb**	absorbed
sect	insects		significant	**sore**	sorely
secu	consecutive		signify		soreness
	execute	**simple**	simplicity		sorer
	execution		simplified		sorest
	executive		simplify	**sorpt**	absorption
	persecute		simplifying	**source**	resourceful
	prosecute		simply	**space**	spacious
	second	**simult**	simultaneous	**spect**	expect
seem	seemed	**sire**	desirability		expectation
self	selfishness		desirable		expected
semi	semicircle		desire		expecting
	semicolon		desirous		inspect
sense	sensible		undesirable		inspection
sent	absent	**sist**	consist		inspector
	consents		consisted		respect
	dissent		consistency		respectable
	present		consistent	**spell**	misspell
	presentation		exist		misspells
	presented		existence		misspelling
	resent		inconsistent		spellings
	resentment		insist	**spend**	spending
	sent		insisted	**sphere**	atmosphere
	sentence		insistent		hemisphere
	sentenced		nonexistent	**spice**	conspicuous
	sentimental		persistent		suspicious

Word Parts

spire	antiperspirant
	conspire
	expire
	inspiration
	inspire
	perspire
	respiration
	spiral
	spirit
	spiritual
spise	despise
spond	respond
sponse	irresponsible
	response
	responsibility
	responsible
	responsive
spont	spontaneous
spot	spotless
	spotted
spray	spray
spy	espionage
	spied
	spy
	spying
sta	constant
	constantly
	distance
	distances
	equidistant
establish	establishment
	instant
	instantaneous
	reestablish
	stability
	stable
	state
	statement
	station
	stationary
	stationery
	substantial
star	starless
start	started
stay	staying
step	step
	stepped
	stepping
stir	stir
	stirred
stop	stopping
store	storage

	stored
	storing
story	historian
	historic
	historical
	history
	prehistoric
	stories
	story
stove	stove
strange	strangely
	strangeness
	stranger
	strangest
strenu	strenuous
strophe	apostrophe
stroy	destroyed
struct	instructor
study	studied
	studies
	study
	studying
stupe	stupendous
	stupid
	stupidity
sturdy	sturdiest
su	suspicious
suade	persuade
suase	persuasion
	persuasive
sub	sub
	subject
	submissive
	submit
	submitted
	subscribe
	subscription
	substantial
suc	succeed
	succeeded
	succeeding
	success
	successful
	unsuccessful
suf	suffer
	suffered
	suffering
sum	summarization
	summarize
	summary
	summation
	summed

	summit
	sums
sume	assumed
	consume
	presume
sumpt	assumption
	consumption
	presumption
sun	sunnier
	sunniest
	sunny
sup	supplies
	supplying
	support
	supported
	suppose
super	superfluous
	supervise
	supervision
	supervisor
sur	surface
	surfaced
	surprise
	surrounding
	survivable
	survive
	survived
	survivor
	survivors
sus	susceptible
	suspend
	suspension
swim	swimmer
	swimmers
	swimming
	swims
sym	symphony
symbol	symbol
	symbolic
	symbolize
	symbols
syn	synonym
	synonymous
tail	curtail
tain	contain
	contained
	container
	entertain
	entertainer
	entertainment
	maintain
	pertaining

take	mistake		thoroughly		tried
	mistaken	**thought**	thought		trying
	mistakes		thoughtful	**tw**	between
	taken	**through**	through		twelve
	takes	**time**	time		twenty
techno	technical	**tinue**	continue		twenty-two
	technique		continued		twice
	technology		continuous		twilight
tect	protected		discontinue		twin
	unprotected	**toy**	toy		twins
teen	fifteen		toys		two
	fourteen	**trace**	trace	**twelf**	twelfth
	fourteenth		traceable	**twelve**	twelve
	nineteen		tracing	**ty**	casualty
tele	telegraph	**tract**	extraction		duty
	telephone		extractor		fifty
	telescope		tract		forties
	televise	**trade**	trades		fortieth
	television		trading		forty
tend	extend	**trans**	transfer		forty-four
	intend		transferred		forty-ninth
tene	tenuous		transform		ninetieth
tense	extension		transformed		ninety
	intensify		transit		ninety-five
tent	discontent		translate		ninety-ninth
ter	deter		translation		safety
	terrible		transmissible		twenty
	terrific		transmission		twenty-two
	terrify		transmit	**ual**	actuality
	terrifying		transmitting		actually
	terror		transplant		casual
th	fifth		transport		casually
	forty-ninth		transporting		casualty
	fourteenth	**trap**	trapped		eventual
	fourth		trapping		individual
	growth	**treme**	tremendous		spiritual
	health		tremor		unusual
	healthier	**tri**	triangle		unusually
	healthy		tricycle		usual
	ninety-ninth		trivial		visual
	ninth	**trim**	trim	**um**	museum
	truth	**trip**	tripped		vacuum
	truthful	**trol**	control	**un**	unaffected
	twelfth		controlled		unappreciative
	unhealthy		controlling		unbreakable
theo	theology		uncontrollable		unconscious
they	they	**true**	true		uncontrollable
thief	thief		truly		uncover
thieve	thievery		truth		undefined
	thieves		truthful		undeniable
think	think	**try**	mistrial		undeniably
thorough	thorough		trial		undesirable

	undiscovered		failure	**vent**	event	
	unenlightened		manufacture		eventual	
	unfixed		manufacturer		invent	
	unforgettable		pleasure	**verse**	conversation	
	unfortunate		pressure		converse	
	unfortunately		procedure		inversion	
	unhappy		puncture		reversal	
	unhealthy		rupture		reverse	
	uninformed	**ury**	luxurious		reversible	
	unjustifiable		luxury		reversion	
	unnoticed	**us**	chorus		universal	
	unoriginal	**use**	reusable		universe	
	unplanned		unusual		versatile	
	unpleasant		unusually		versatility	
	unprotected		usable		verse	
	unquestionable		usage		version	
	unreported		useful	**vert**	advertise	
	unsuccessful		usual		convertible	
	unusual	**ute**	consecutive	**very**	verification	
	unusually		execute		verified	
une	fortunate		execution		verify	
	fortune		executive		very	
	misfortune		persecute	**vet**	vet	
	opportune		prosecute	**via**	deviate	
	opportunities	**vacu**	evacuate		deviation	
	opportunity		evacuated		obvious	
	unfortunate		vacancy		obviously	
	unfortunately		vacant		previous	
uni	reunion		vacate		trivial	
	reunite		vacation		viaduct	
	unanimous		vacuous	**vice**	advice	
	unanimously		vacuum		vice	
	unicycle	**vade**	invade		vicious	
	unification	**vale**	equivalence		viciousness	
	unified		equivalent	**vide**	divide	
	uniform		valid		divided	
	unify	**value**	valuable		divider	
	union		valueless		individual	
	unique	**van**	van		provide	
	uniqueness	**vant**	advantage	**view**	previewing	
	unison		advantageous		reviewer	
	unit		disadvantage	**vince**	convincible	
	unite	**vary**	variability		invincible	
	united		variable	**virtue**	virtue	
	unity		variance		virtuous	
	universal		varied	**vise**	advise	
	universe		variety		advised	
uous	conspicuous		various		devise	
	tenuous		varying		divisible	
up	whereupon	**veal**	reveal		division	
ure	creature	**vase**	invasion		invisible	
	enclosure	**vele**	revelation		provision	

Word Parts

	revised	**white**	whitest
	revision	**who**	whoever
	supervise	**whole**	whole
	supervision		wholesome
	supervisor	**whom**	whomever
	televise	**wide**	widest
	television	**wife**	wife
	visibility	**winter**	winter
	visible	**wit**	wittier
	vision		wittiest
	visit		witty
	visitor	**wive**	wives
	visitors	**wolf**	wolf
	visual	**wolve**	wolverine
vive	revival		wolves
	revived	**wonder**	wonderful
	survivable		wondrous
	survive	**work**	worker
	survived		workers
	survivor		working
	vivacious	**worry**	worried
	vivid		worrisome
voice	voice		worry
vole	benevolent		worrying
	malevolent	**wrap**	wrapper
volve	involvement		wrappers
	revolve		wrapping
	revolver		wrappings
vote	voter		wraps
wait	wait	**write**	write
	waited		writer
	waiter	**year**	yearly
ware	warehouses		years
wash	washer		
waste	waste		
	wasteful		
wax	waxier		
	waxiest		
	waxy		
weak	weak		
	weaker		
week	weeks		
weigh	weigh		
	weighed		
	weight		
wel	welcome		
were	were		
what	whatever		
	whatsoever		
when	when		
where	whereas		
	whereupon		

Study Lists

1-5

acquire
across
action
airport
autobiography
autograph
barely
biography
changing
decided
deport
discontent
expensive
export
exports
famous
final
forgiven
formal
fortunate
graphic
great
greatly
hopeful
hopelessly
hoping
imagination
important
informal
inquire
introduce
lately
likely
likeness
lovely
misinformed
misjudged
misspell
mistaken
morphograph
performance
photographer

photographic
portable
porter
really
reformed
replacement
replacing
report
reported
require
requirement
reusable
should
showed
support
supported
telegraph
television
their
tracing
transform
translate
transmit
transplant
transport
transporting
uncover
uninformed
unreported
usable
usage
widest
wonderful

6-10

admirable
admire
amusement
athletic
athletically
baggage
basement
basic

bibliography
changing
civilize
confusing
conscientious
critically
criticism
deduction
dispel
excessively
expressive
formless
geography
gotten
graphite
hats
hopeless
hottest
inquiring
interest
inversion
knots
madness
magic
medicine
notice
package
partial
parting
patting
people
perceptive
photograph
photography
physicist
placing
pleasure
poisonous
pulsate
realize
sadness
sitting
snapped
spotted

starless
storage
stranger
surprise
swimmer
telescope
trades
trading
translation
transmission
tripped
valuable
valueless
washer
whitest

11-15

acknowledge
admission
advised
appearance
appeared
baggage
bagging
beautiful
blameless
buried
careless
carriage
copied
covered
crying
denial
devise
diseased
drying
easy
embarrassed
enjoyment
failure
fanciest
fateful
fatty

friendly
glorious
haphazard
happen
happiness
happy
heaviest
hurrying
impartial
improved
incurable
joyous
judging
justice
leakage
leaked
leaking
manufacture
married
mishap
mishaps
mistake
mistakes
movement
packed
packing
perhaps
pitiful
planning
playful
racing
refining
revision
runner
runny
sadder
saddest
sadly
saying
shiny
shipped
shipping
shopper
skinny

232 Study Lists

Study Lists

slammed
sorely
soreness
sorer
sorest
staying
stepped
stored
storing
strangely
strangeness
strangest
studying
sturdiest
televise
thoroughly
toys
trial
tried
trying
unusually
varied
version
vision
visitor
worried

16-20

accommodate
admit
athletics
baker
bakes
baking
boxer
burial
business
casual
commit
commitment
compelling
copying
denying

embarrassment
enjoyed
fitness
friendliest
happier
happiest
happily
hazardous
hidden
imaginary
improvement
informative
inquired
invisible
luckier
luckiest
lucky
manufacturer
mothering
noisier
omit
paragraph
permit
pleasant
propel
receive
repellent
shopping
shops
skipped
sprayed
stopping
sunnier
sunniest
sunny
supervision
swimming
swims
unfixed
unpleasant
usual
wittier
wittiest
witty

worrisome
wrapper
wrapping
wraps

21-25

accommodation
actually
another
applied
astronomer
biggest
casualty
commodity
complying
concur
consistent
critic
critical
currency
current
durable
duration
during
endurance
endure
fantasies
fantasy
funny
hemisphere
imagine
inconsistent
knotted
likelihood
misfortune
model
moderate
modern
modernize
modest
occasion
occasionally
occur

philosopher
planned
recur
rephrased
stepping
stirred
various
visit
worrying

26-30

admittance
advise
allotment
allotted
allowed
anchored
approach
backache
begin
beginner
beginning
characteristic
chemical
chemistry
chords
chorus
committee
controlled
curtail
differ
disaster
disciple
discipline
echoes
excel
excelled
excellence
excellent
exercising
ferry
forbid
forbidden

forgive
forgot
forgotten
forsake
forsaken
growth
healthy
industrial
knowledge
loneliness
marriage
mechanical
mechanism
melancholy
military
modesty
occurrence
offer
omitted
origin
original
permitting
plants
preferred
propeller
propelling
purse
recurring
refer
safety
schematic
schooling
sound
suffer
technology
transfer
transferred
uncontrollable
unhappy
very
visual

Study Lists

31-35

anonymous
belligerent
benediction
bicycle
businesses
citation
concurred
concurrence
concurs
conductor
contradict
contradiction
controlling
dictation
dictator
diction
dictionary
disappoint
disciplinary
edict
educate
familiar
forth
hymnal
hyphenated
hysterical
impersonal
impersonate
indict
indictment
magician
malediction
manage
manual
manuscript
mysterious
mystical
occurred
occurs
personality
personalize
personify

physician
predict
prediction
probable
production
question
rebellion
received
receiver
recommended
recurred
recurrence
recurrent
recurs
reduced
regrettable
rhythmical
site
surrounding
symbolic
synonym
synonymous
unforgettable
unquestionable

36-40

acknowledged
activity
adequate
admitting
appearing
beam
bridge
characterization
close
compelled
conceivable
conception
create
deceive
deceived
deceptive
density

describe
description
discoveries
earlier
enduring
equal
equation
equator
equidistant
equinox
equivalent
find
forties
fortieth
forty
forty-one
four
fourteen
fourteenth
fourth
fury
hole
importance
importing
indescribable
inquiry
inscribe
inscription
list
misconceive
misconception
mystery
opportunity
perceive
perception
performing
permissible
predictable
preferring
prescribe
prescription
rebels
receptive
recommend

regretful
rejection
scripture
separate
story
submissive
submit
subscribe
subscription
summarization
summarize
summary
summation
summed
summit
sums
unenlightened
variance
varying
weak
yearly

41-45

antecedent
asterisk
breathlessness
clothes
conversation
created
creation
creature
descriptive
earliest
enclosure
exceed
exceeded
excessive
furious
healthier
inconceivable
indispensable
infuriate
involvement

mysteriously
observation
perceived
precede
precedence
prepared
prescriptive
presentation
previewing
proceed
quotation
raining
recede
reception
referring
refusal
remarried
semicolon
simply
stories
succeed

46-50

concede
conceded
concedes
dictionaries
divide
exceeding
exceedingly
exercises
familiarize
individual
meaningless
meant
omissions
opposite
preceded
precedent
preceding
procedure
proceeded
proceeding

234 Study Lists

Study Lists

proceedings
receding
remittance
resentment
reservation
rhetoric
rheumatism
rhinoceros
rhubarb
rhyme
rhymed
rhyming
rhythm
rhythmic
scheming
sentence
succeeded
succeeding
surfaced
symphony
transit
transmitting
weight
weighted

51-55

affect
between
clouds
coarse
compare
confined
constant
contrary
define
definite
definitely
definition
deviate
distance
equate
event
eventual

finally
finish
finite
indefinite
indefinitely
infinite
instant
manicure
manifestation
manipulate
mismanage
obvious
opportune
pressure
previous
profess
puncture
sacred
sacrifice
sacrificial
sacrilege
sacrilegious
sentenced
stable
state
statement
station
surface
trivial
twelve
twenty
twice
twilight
twin
undefined
viaduct
weather

56-60

advice
armor/armour
behavior/
    behaviour

center/centre
color/colour
conclusive
emigrate
equally
establish
evacuate
favor/favour
favorite/favourite
glamor/glamour
gray/grey
harbor/harbour
honor/honour
humor/humour
immigrant
immigrate
labor/labour
migrant
migrate
migratory
mold/mould
museum
music
neighbor/
    neighbour
obviously
odor/odour
patriarch
patriot
patriotic
patron
patronage
patronize
plough/plow
principal
program/
    programme
punctual
punctuate
radial
radiant
radiate
radiation
radioactive

radiology
reversal
sacrament
studied
telephone
tire/tyre
vacancy
vacant
vacate
vacuous
vacuum
valor/valour
vapor/vapour
variable

61-65

aisle
benefactor
beneficial
benefit
benevolent
benign
carrying
classified
classify
clearance
coarsely
departmental
equivalence
expedient
expedition
falsify
horrify
identify
impediment
intensify
justify
malady
malice
malicious
malignant
managerial
modify

musician
mystify
nutrient
nutriment
nutrition
nutritious
pedal
pedestrian
pedicure
qualify
reaction
reestablish
reporter
sale
signify
simplicity
simplified
simplify
simplifying
stationery
terrify
two
unjustifiable

66-70

acquainted
acquired
acquittal
acquitted
affection
autobiographical
autobiography
cautious
challenge
classifying
compete
competition
competitor
competitors
conscience
conscious
conspicuous
continued

Study Lists

continuous
deviation
disappearance
equipment
equipped
espionage
expedite
experience
experiment
fort
gracious
graciousness
identified
inexperienced
knight
migration
noncommittal
office
official
peril
quieted
quitter
quitting
quizzed
quizzical
quoted
sandwich
sandwiches
science
scientific
scientist
spacious
spied
strenuous
tract
vacation
verse
vicious
virtue
virtuous

71-75

accounted
accounting
acquiring
application
apply
applying
central
compliance
comply
concentrate
counted
counting
curious
decentralize
deluxe
dislocate
eccentric
entertain
fortify
grammar
injection
local
locate
location
locomotive
luxurious
luxury
maintain
multiply
objective
pertaining
profession
programmer
programming
project
projection
projector
quizzing
refused
rejected
relocate

replica
separation
subject
successful
tenuous
unprotected
viciousness

76-80

absent
affectionate
appliance
beggar
elevation
enumerate
experimental
identifying
innumerable
irrelevant
lever
manually
marrying
nervous
numeral
numerical
numerous
pair
pliable
relevance
relevant
ridicule
ridiculed
ridiculous
suspicious
tremendous
tremor
unsuccessful
wait
waiter
waste
wasteful
weighed
wholesome

81-85

abrupt
abruptly
agonize
applicant
bankrupt
beautify
caravan
categorize
certificate
certifying
competent
container
correctly
corrupt
corruption
course
deter
effect
entertainment
eruption
exam
examination
examine
friendliness
glorify
gymnasium
historian
historic
history
implying
influenza
inspection
inspector
interrupt
laboratory
multiplying
objectionable
opportunities
pacifist
robberies
rupture

sight
submarine
terrible
terrific
terrifying
terror
unconscious
undeniable
unicycle
uniform
union
unite
verify
veterinarian

86-90

affluent
bicyclist
bilateral
burying
caution
certain
certify
complicate
concert
cyclic
cyclone
disruptive
effective
effort
effortless
equilateral
fluent
fluid
historical
influence
interruption
justification
lateral
multiplication
pacifying
prehistoric
reunite

Study Lists

spying
superfluous
supplying
tricycle
unaffected
unanimous
unification
unify
unique
unison
unit
unity
universal
universe
versatile
versatility

91-95

accompaniment
animal
antagonize
antibodies
antibody
antiperspirant
antisocial
antonym
categories
cautions
certification
certified
companies
compensate
consistency
denied
fluently
identification
influential
insistent
isle
judgment/
    judgement
judicial
judicious

justifiable
justified
misjudge
precaution
prejudge
prejudice
prejudicial
principle
respectable
reunion
significant
stationary
studies
substantial
unified
verification
verified

96-100

appreciable
appreciate
apprehensive
automotive
commotion
comprehension
conclusion
consecutive
conservation
conspire
decision
defensive
demote
depreciate
division
erosion
except
excite
exclusive
execute
execution
exist
existence
expand

expansion
expect
expectation
expense
expire
explosive
extension
inclusive
insisted
inspiration
invasion
motion
motive
motor
offensive
originate
persecute
persistent
persuasion
philosophical
precious
professional
promote
promotion
prosecute
provision
remote
respiration
responsive
second
spirit
spiritual
suspension
too
unappreciative
week
whole

101-105

advantageous
antique
audible
believable

believe
changeable
chargeable
compatible
conclude
considerable
consist
courageous
critique
divider
exchangeable
excitable
exclamation
exclude
explanation
extraction
five
horrible
include
incredible
insist
inspire
knives
knowledgeable
manageable
mystique
noticeable
outrageous
physique
possible
proclamation
relieve
repetition
revelation
serviceable
susceptible
technique
thieves
traceable
transmissible
visible
wolves
workable

106-110

absorb
absorption
administration
angry
anxiety
associate
association
assume
assumption
authority
collaborate
confer
conference
conferred
conferring
consider
considerably
consideration
considers
consume
consumption
deduce
deodorize
desirable
desire
desires
desirous
differed
different
differing
disastrous
dissociate
elaborate
entered
entrance
entry
evaporate
extraneous
formality
forty-ninth
glamorize

Study Lists

hindrance
humanity
humorous
hungrily
hungry
inconsiderate
inference
inferred
inferring
instantaneous
introduction
laborious
miscellaneous
monstrous
nine
nineteen
nineteenth
ninetieth
ninety
ninety-five
ninth
offered
offering
preferable
preference
presume
presumption
product
propriety
reality
reduce
reduction
reference
referral
referred
registration
rigorous
simultaneous
sociable
social
societies
society
spontaneous
suffered

suffering
twenty-ninth
undesirable
vaporize
variety
wondrous

111–115

actual
actuality
adhere
adhered
adherent
adhesive
analogy
anthropology
apologize
applicable
astrology
audience
audition
author
biology
capable
capacity
chronology
coherent
cohesive
conquer
credible
deception
deniable
entomology
fifty
forty-four
geology
hesitant
hesitate
hospitable
hospital
hospitality
human
humid

humidity
incoherent
irritable
irritate
legal
legality
logic
major
majority
morphology
nineteen
originality
ornithology
prefers
prior
priority
psychology
replaceable
sociology
stupid
stupidity
theology

116–120

advertise
apology
argument
authorization
authorize
awful
awfully
chastise
compatibility
compressible
compression
computerize
corruptible
curiosity
deductible
deductive
desirability
difference
disability

duly
durability
duty
exhaustible
exhaustion
exhaustive
formalize
generosity
geologist
hospitalize
legalize
monstrosity
organization
organize
possibility
prefer
probability
resistible
resistive
responsibility
responsible
reversible
reversion
revival
revive
sensible
stability
survivable
survive
survivor
truly
truth
truthful
visibility
vivacious
vivid

Spelling Rules

Lesson	Rule	Explanation
3	**Final-E Rule**	When do you drop the final **e** from a word? When the next morphograph begins with a vowel letter.
7	**Doubling Rule (Short Words)**	When do you double the final **c** when a short word? When the word ends **cvc** and the next morphograph begins with **v.**
12	**Y-to-I Rule**	When do you change the **y** to **i** in a word? When a word ends with a consonant-and-**y** and the next morphograph begins with anything except **i.**
28	**Doubling Rule (Long Words)**	When a word ends in a short **cvc** morphograph use the doubling rule.
51	**Final-Vowel Rule (Part 1)**	*There are two parts to this rule. The first part of the rule is introduced in Lesson 51:* Drop the final vowel from a morphograph when the next morphograph begins with a vowel. *This rule covers morphographs that end in* **e,** *such as* **muse + ic = music.** *It also covers other vowels:* **vacu + ate = vacate.**
58	**Final-Vowel Rule (Part 2)**	*In Lesson 58 the second part of the final-vowel rule is given:* Drop the final vowel when the next morphograph begins with a vowel UNLESS YOU HEAR BOTH VOWEL SOUNDS. *In the word* **museum** *you hear the vowels* **e** *and* **u,** *so you keep the final vowel,* **e.** *In the word* **evacuate,** *you hear the vowels* **u** *and* **a,** *so you keep the final vowel,* **u.**
84	**Final-Vowel Rule (Final Y)**	Drop the final **y** when a word ends consonant-and-**y** and the next morphograph begins with **i,** unless you hear both vowel sounds. *In the word* **crying,** *you hear the vowel for* **y** *and for* **i,** *so you keep the final vowel,* **y.** *In* **glory + ify = glorify,** *you cannot hear both vowels, so the* **y** *drops.*
97	**E-X Rule**	Drop the **s** from the beginning of a morphograph when that morphograph follows **ex.**
107	**F-E-R Doubling Rule**	Double the **r** if **fer** is stressed. *In the word* **referred,** **fer** *is stressed, so you double the* **r.** *In the word* **reference,** **fer** *is not stressed, so you don't double the* **r.**
112	**I-T-Y Rule**	Drop the **u** when you combine **ous + ity = osity.** Add an **i** when you combine **able + ity = ability.** Add an **i** when you combine **ible + ity = ibility.**

Facts About Morphographs

1. All morphographs follow spelling rules.
2. All morphographs have meaning.
3. Morphographs are the smallest word parts that have meaning.
4. Some words have only one morphograph.
   Some words have more than one morphograph.

	1	2	3	4	5	6
A	re**port**	photo**graph**ic	in**quire**	trans**form**	**trans**plant	re**tain**
B	im**port**ed	**graph**	ac**quire**	**form**al	**trans**mit	con**tain**er
C	**port**	tele**graph**	re**quire**ment	unin**form**ed	**trans**porting	ob**tain**able
D				per**form**ance	**trans**late	enter**tain**

Contractions

Component Words	Contractions	Component Words	Contractions
are not	aren't	that is	that's
can not	can't	they are	they're
could not	couldn't	they had	they'd
did not	didn't	they have	they've
do not	don't	they will	they'll
does not	doesn't	was not	wasn't
have not	haven't	we are	we're
he had	he'd	we had	we'd
he is	he's	we have	we've
he will	he'll	we will	we'll
here is	here's	were not	weren't
I am	I'm	what is	what's
I will	I'll	who is	who's
it is	it's	would not	wouldn't
let us	let's	you are	you're
she had	she'd	you had	you'd
she is	she's	you have	you've
she will	she'll	you will	you'll
should not	shouldn't		

Homonyms

affect   refers to: make something change
example: The coarse clouds will *affect* the weather.

effect   refers to: outcome
example: The moon has an *effect* on the tides.

---

aisle   refers to: a row
example: The suitcase was blocking the *aisle*.

I'll   refers to: I will
example: *I'll* be there at noon.

isle   refers to: an island
example: Let's move to a tropical *isle*.

---

ate   refers to: eat in the past
example: I *ate* a sandwich.

eight   refers to: the number 8
example: The dog had *eight* puppies.

---

bare   refers to: without covering; empty
example: In the winter some trees are *bare*.

bear   refers to: a certain animal or to support
example: The huge *bear* drank from a stream.
example: The bridge can't *bear* more weight.

---

close   refers to: shut something
example: Please *close* the door.

clothes   refers to: things you wear
example: They bought lots of *clothes*.

---

coarse   refers to: rough and ragged
example: The old dog's fur was *coarse*.

course   refers to: path or route you follow
example: The plane changed *course* because of the storm.

---

desert   refers to: leave or abandon
example: I wouldn't *desert* a friend in need.

dessert   refers to: food served at the end of a meal
example: We had ice cream for *dessert*.

---

feat   refers to: something hard to do
example: Climbing the mountain was a great *feat*.

feet   refers to: body part
example: Her *feet* were sore from running.

---

for   refers to: in place of
example: She went to the store *for* me.

four   refers to: the number 4
example: Cats have *four* legs.

---

hear   refers to: listen
example: I can't *hear* you.

here   refers to: this place
example: Come over *here*.

---

hole   refers to: empty space
example: I have a *hole* in my sock.

whole   refers to: entire; complete
example: He ate the *whole* pie.

Homonyms

it's refers to: it is
example: *It's* raining

its refers to: belonging to it
example: The dog chased *its* tale.

---

loan refers to: allow to borrow something
example: She will *loan* me lunch money.

lone refers to: by itself
example: There was a *lone* tree.

---

marry refers to: wed or unite
example: She said she would *marry* Steve.

merry refers to: happy, full of fun
example: The hikers were a *merry* group.

---

meat refers to: food from animals
example: Some people don't eat *meat.*

meet refers to: come together
example: We agreed to *meet* next week.

---

no refers to: negative answer
example: *No,* I'm not going.

know refers to: understand or be familiar with
example: We *know* how to sail.

---

peace refers to: calm; no war
example: I like *peace* and quiet.

piece refers to: a part
example: I ate a *piece* of fruit.

---

pear refers to: a certain fruit that grows on a tree
example: Mom put a *pear* in my lunch.

pair refers to: two of a kind
example: Mack got a new *pair* of basketball shoes.

---

plain refers to: simple; ordinary
example: She wore a *plain* black dress.

plane refers to: flat surface or air transportation
example: The *plane* landed safely.

---

principal refers to: the person who runs a school
example: Our *principal* keeps the school running smoothly.

principle refers to: a rule
example: Telling the truth is an important *principle.*

---

right refers to: correct or opposite of left
example: All my answers were *right.*
example: She wears a ring on her *right* hand.

write refers to: put words on paper
example: You must *write* neatly.

Homonyms

sail	refers to:	travel on water in a ship or a boat
	example:	We learned how to *sail* at camp.
sale	refers to:	available to buy, or an offer at a cheaper price
	example:	Our house is for *sale*.
	example:	He bought the shoes on *sale*.
scene	refers to:	view or setting
	example:	It was a painting of an ocean *scene*.
seen	refers to:	see in the past
	example:	I have *seen* that picture.
sew	refers to:	join with a needle and thread
	example:	He will *sew* a new button on his coat.
sow	refers to:	plant seeds
	example:	Farmers *sow* their fields in the early spring.
site	refers to:	place or location
	example:	We are building a house on this *site*.
sight	refers to:	seeing, vision or view
	example:	A dog's sense of smell is better than its sense of *sight*.
some	refers to:	not all; an indefinite number
	example:	*Some* of my friends were there.
sum	refers to:	the total amount
	example:	The *sum* of two and ten is twelve.

stationary	refers to:	something that doesn't move
	example:	She exercises on a *stationary* bike.
stationery	refers to:	paper for writing letters
	example:	His *stationery* had his address on it.
tail	refers to:	the back end
	example:	The dog chased his *tail*.
tale	refers to:	a story
	example:	He told an interesting *tale*.
their	refers to:	belonging to them
	example:	It is *their* house.
there	refers to:	that place
	example:	Go over *there*.
they're	refers to:	they are
	example:	I think *they're* ready.
threw	refers to:	throw in the past
	example:	She *threw* the ball.
through	refers to:	in one side and out the other
	example:	We went *through* the tunnel.
to	refers to:	at or toward
	example:	She walked *to* school.
too	refers to:	also
	example:	Why don't you come along, *too*?
two	refers to:	the number 2
	example:	I ate *two* apples.

Homonyms

vary	refers to: change		**weak**	refers to: the opposite of strong
	example: His moods *vary* from day to day.			example: The wrestler felt *weak* after the match.
very	refers to: really, quite, especially		**week**	refers to: seven days
	example: That story is *very* imaginative.			example: We go on vacation next *week*.

waist   refers to: a person's mid-section
            example: She wore a belt around her *waist*.

waste   refers to: throw away
            example: Don't *waste* the food.

wait   refers to: delay or expect something
            example: We had to *wait* an hour for the bus.

weight   refers to: heaviness
            example: He felt like he had the *weight* of the world on his shoulders.

ware   refers to: product for sale
            example: The baker sold his *wares*.

wear   refers to: have clothes on your body
            example: What shall I *wear* today?

where   refers to: what place
            example: *Where* do you want to go?

weather   refers to: what it feels like out of doors
            example: Always wear a hat cold *weather*.

whether   refers to: if
            example: I don't care *whether* I go or not.

wood   refers to: what trees are made of
            example: We need *wood* for the fire.

would   refers to: what might happen
            example: I *would* like to go to Paris.

your   refers to: belonging to you
            example: *Your* coat is blue.

you're   refers to: you are
            example: *You're* early.

Test Charts

	Lesson 5	Lesson 10	Lesson 15	Lesson 20	Lesson 25	Lesson 30	30-Lesson Total
Super Speller	25	25	25	25	25	25	
	24	24	24	24	24	24	
	23	23	23	23	23	23	138 = Super Speller
Very Good Speller	22	22	22	22	22	22	
	21	21	21	21	21	21	
	20	20	20	20	20	20	
	19	19	19	19	19	19	
	18	18	18	18	18	18	
	17	17	17	17	17	17	
	16	16	16	16	16	16	
	15	15	15	15	15	15	
	14	14	14	14	14	14	
	13	13	13	13	13	13	
	12	12	12	12	12	12	
	11	11	11	11	11	11	
	10	10	10	10	10	10	
	9	9	9	9	9	9	
	8	8	8	8	8	8	
	7	7	7	7	7	7	
	6	6	6	6	6	6	
	5	5	5	5	5	5	
	4	4	4	4	4	4	
	3	3	3	3	3	3	
	2	2	2	2	2	2	
	1	1	1	1	1	1	

Test Charts

	Lesson 35	Lesson 40	Lesson 45	Lesson 50	Lesson 55	Lesson 60	30-Lesson Total
Super Speller	25	25	25	25	25	25	
	24	24	24	24	24	24	
	23	23	23	23	23	23	138 = Super Speller
Very Good Speller	22	22	22	22	22	22	
	21	21	21	21	21	21	
	20	20	20	20	20	20	
	19	19	19	19	19	19	
	18	18	18	18	18	18	
	17	17	17	17	17	17	
	16	16	16	16	16	16	
	15	15	15	15	15	15	
	14	14	14	14	14	14	
	13	13	13	13	13	13	
	12	12	12	12	12	12	
	11	11	11	11	11	11	
	10	10	10	10	10	10	
	9	9	9	9	9	9	
	8	8	8	8	8	8	
	7	7	7	7	7	7	
	6	6	6	6	6	6	
	5	5	5	5	5	5	
	4	4	4	4	4	4	
	3	3	3	3	3	3	
	2	2	2	2	2	2	
	1	1	1	1	1	1	

Test Charts

	Lesson 65	Lesson 70	Lesson 75	Lesson 80	Lesson 85	Lesson 90	30-Lesson Total
Super Speller	25	25	25	25	25	25	
	24	24	24	24	24	24	
	23	23	23	23	23	23	
Very Good Speller	22	22	22	22	22	22	**138 = Super Speller**
	21	21	21	21	21	21	
	20	20	20	20	20	20	
	19	19	19	19	19	19	
	18	18	18	18	18	18	
	17	17	17	17	17	17	
	16	16	16	16	16	16	
	15	15	15	15	15	15	
	14	14	14	14	14	14	
	13	13	13	13	13	13	
	12	12	12	12	12	12	
	11	11	11	11	11	11	
	10	10	10	10	10	10	
	9	9	9	9	9	9	
	8	8	8	8	8	8	
	7	7	7	7	7	7	
	6	6	6	6	6	6	
	5	5	5	5	5	5	
	4	4	4	4	4	4	
	3	3	3	3	3	3	
	2	2	2	2	2	2	
	1	1	1	1	1	1	

Test Charts

	Lesson 95	Lesson 100	Lesson 105	Lesson 110	Lesson 115	Lesson 120	30-Lesson Total
Super Speller	25	25	25	25	25	25	
	24	24	24	24	24	24	
	23	23	23	23	23	23	138 = Super Speller
Very Good Speller	22	22	22	22	22	22	
	21	21	21	21	21	21	
	20	20	20	20	20	20	
	19	19	19	19	19	19	
	18	18	18	18	18	18	
	17	17	17	17	17	17	
	16	16	16	16	16	16	
	15	15	15	15	15	15	
	14	14	14	14	14	14	
	13	13	13	13	13	13	
	12	12	12	12	12	12	
	11	11	11	11	11	11	
	10	10	10	10	10	10	
	9	9	9	9	9	9	
	8	8	8	8	8	8	
	7	7	7	7	7	7	
	6	6	6	6	6	6	
	5	5	5	5	5	5	
	4	4	4	4	4	4	
	3	3	3	3	3	3	
	2	2	2	2	2	2	
	1	1	1	1	1	1	